P9-DCH-025

BOOK SALE

Additional praise for *The Art of Misdiagnosis*

"Riveting, insightful, and beautifully written, this memoir kept me up all night."

—CHRISTINA BAKER KLINE,
New York Times best-selling author of *Orphan Train*

"Gayle Brandeis dances on the edge of memory's razor: both candid and eloquent, *The Art of Misdiagnosis* never fails to cut down to the truth. I was both moved and enlightened by this unflinching memoir."

—LINDA GRAY SEXTON,
best-selling author of *Searching for Mercy Street:
My Journey Back to My Mother, Anne Sexton,*
and *Half in Love: Surviving the Legacy of Suicide*

"Gayle Brandeis is one of the smartest and most compassionate voices in nonfiction today. Her insights about how we live as women, as mothers and daughters, and as human beings cut straight to the heart. Everyone needs to read her."

—HOPE EDELMAN,
internationally best-selling author of *Motherless Daughters*

"Deeply compassionate, and breathtakingly brave, Brandeis's memoir is a raw, unflinching trip down a rabbit hole, unspooling both the chaotic life of her mentally unbalanced mother and how her mother's obsession with physical illness crash-landed Brandeis's own life—and health—from girlhood to marriage and motherhood. About the stories we desperately need to make of our lives in order to survive, and how the body sometimes speaks what the mind dares not, this is also an extraordinarily moving portrait of a troubled mother and of the daughter who fearlessly, poetically, writes her way into discovering her truest self. Truthfully, I am in awe."

—CAROLINE LEAVITT,
New York Times best-selling author
of *Is This Tomorrow* and *Pictures of You*

"*The Art of Misdiagnosis* is Gayle Brandeis's masterpiece, and it reads with the urgency of a literary thriller. Here Brandeis delves into the liminal place—between life and death, between psychosis and sanity, between love and guilt—with a poet's heart and a detective's courage. If you've ever watched someone you love unravel, or if you've asked the echoing 'why?' of suicide, you'll find home in these pages."

—ARIEL GORE,
author of *The End of Eve*

The Art of Misdiagnosis

The Art of Misdiagnosis

A Memoir

Gayle Brandeis

Beacon Press
Boston

BEACON PRESS
Boston, Massachusetts
www.beacon.org

Beacon Press books
are published under the auspices of
the Unitarian Universalist Association of Congregations.

20 19 18 17   8 7 6 5 4 3 2 1

This book is printed on acid-free paper that meets the uncoated paper
ANSI/NISO specifications for permanence as revised in 1992.

Text design and composition by Kim Arney

In some cases, names and other identifying characteristics of people
mentioned in this work have been changed to protect their identities.

Portions of this memoir appeared, in different form, in *Full Grown People*, the
Manifest-Station, *Midnight Breakfast*, the *Nervous Breakdown*, the *Rumpus*, *Salon*,
She Writes, and the *Saranac Review*.

Library of Congress Cataloging-in-Publication Data

Names: Brandeis, Gayle, author.
Title: The art of misdiagnosis : a memoir / Gayle Brandeis.
Description: Boston, Massachusetts : Beacon Press, [2017]
Identifiers: LCCN 2017002002 (print) | LCCN 2017029234 (ebook) |
   ISBN 9780807044902 (e-book) | ISBN 9780807044865 (hardback)
Subjects: LCSH: Brandeis, Gayle—Mental health. | Schizophrenics—Family
   relationships—Biography. | Suicide victims—Biography. | Mother and
   child—Biography. | BISAC: BIOGRAPHY & AUTOBIOGRAPHY /
   Personal Memoirs. | PSYCHOLOGY / Psychopathology / Schizophrenia. |
   PSYCHOLOGY / Suicide.
Classification: LCC RC514 (ebook) | LCC RC514 .B676 2017 (print) |
   DDC 616.89/80092 [B] —dc23
LC record available at https://lccn.loc.gov/2017002002

. . . .

In loving memory of Arlene June Baylen Brandeis,

1939–2009

DO YOU HAVE ANY OF THESE SYMPTOMS?

Joint pain

Gum disease

Detached retina, in early or midlife

Mitral valve prolapse

Family history of sudden cardiac death

Crohn's disease

Irritable bowel syndrome

Constipation

Hypermobile joints

Skin hyperextensibility

Unexplained regurgitation or vomiting

Sensitive to sunlight

Nervous when dieting

Bingeing on carbohydrates

Intermittent psychotic episodes

Severe abdominal pains

Rashes

WE ALL NEED AND DESERVE A CORRECT DIAGNOSIS

—From *The Art of Misdiagnosis:*
An Art Tour into the Genetic History of the Artist
(DVD, back cover; Arlene Baylen Brandeis,
executive producer)

The Art of Misdiagnosis

Prologue

DECEMBER 2009

After my mom hangs herself, I become Nancy Drew. I am looking for clues, for evidence. Answers. I put on a detective hat so I won't have to wear my daughter hat, so I can bear combing through her house. I wrap my new baby to my chest with a bolt of green fabric—my baby born exactly one week before my mom's death—and recommence the dig.

When my sister and I first ventured into our mom's bedroom the day of her memorial, Elizabeth said the space was a perfect metaphor for our mom—lovely and elegant on the surface, total chaos underneath. In the end, our mom couldn't hide the disarray; everything had spilled out, spilled over. Papers were strewn on every surface, leaking out from under her brocade-swathed bed. I bent down that day and found an old Mother's Day card I had written as a teenager, one that gushed about how she was "forever doing things to make me well." I cringe to see it now.

My sister has just flown home to Toronto; it's harder to sift through everything without her here. In the first folder I open after she leaves, I discover notes our mom had taken during a workshop on the seasons of grief. A surprised little laugh kicks in my throat; she's left a guidebook of sorts. The first season, according to her notes, is the "Season of Grieving." Her notes say "Shock—shipwreck of our soul. Disbelief—Lost. Didn't know the world anymore.

You just don't fit anyplace. The true 'you' is not present." Okay, I can relate. The baby on my chest is a life vest; without him, I would be sinking.

I read on to see what I have to look forward to. The second season, her notes tell me, is "Season of the Death of the Soul": "Enter into a landscape for which there are no maps. Walk into the long dark night with no guarantee to find your way out. We must learn to wait without hope. We may hope for the wrong things." Great. Can't wait.

Next comes "Third season of mourning"—"We grieve because we have dared to love and we grieve because we dare to love again. Love is the most difficult task of all, but all is a preparation for love. Fear of loss makes loving so difficult. Death is the bride of love." Death doesn't seem like a bride to me. Death seems more like a gangster, a gangster of love, and not the Steve Miller, space cowboy kind—this is the ruthless, brutal, kind, the kind with complete disregard for decorum. A bride leaves pastel, sugar-coated almonds on the table; a gangster leaves blood.

In the fourth season, we are supposed to "Open to the larger story that grief can interrupt." "Creation of a compassionate heart," her notes say. "Our wounds open us up to others, not only to other people, but to all of creation." Maybe someday I'll get there.

I keep digging.

I find a picture of my mom and Eli, the love of her life, her sister Rochelle's psychiatrist, the married man she loved from the time she was sixteen until he died of cancer ten years later. I've never seen him before; she had always described him as dashing, magnetic, but he looks like a bulbous old lech. His arm is around her in the little black and white snapshot tucked into an old address book—she is radiant, so happy; he looks so happy, too, his arm around a beautiful teenage girl, claiming her when she couldn't claim him, although her oldest sister Sylvia told me she knew about the relationship; she said there was an energy around the two of them when the family went to visit Rochelle in the psychiatric ward.

My mom had told me Eli was the brother of a Supreme Court justice, but when I look up the judge in *Wikipedia*, I can't find any mention of a brother named Eli. I do find an article about Eli in the archives of the *Chicago Tribune*, however—an article that says he had been kidnapped and held for a sizable ransom, that says he had escaped. It appears to have happened the year they met. Is that what made my mom fall in love with him? Is that what led to her obsession with large sums of cash? I find a note about an independent-study high school she briefly attended on Michigan Avenue. I follow a hunch and look up Eli's old office address. Michigan Avenue, too. Had he arranged for her to go there? Did they sneak off together during lunch breaks?

Nancy Drew, Nancy Drew, Nancy Drew.

Asher has fallen asleep. I unknot the wrap from my body, lay him gently on my mom's bed. He stirs a moment; I let him nurse for a few sips until he nods off again. The pale green fabric unfurled next to him is super long—at least four yards. It could easily be used as a noose. Asher has never rolled over in his life, but I imagine him rolling across the bed, looping the heavy cotton around his neck. I gather up the wrap and set it on the end table. When I stand, my shirt is plastered to my chest with sweat and milk. I stretch it forward, let the air touch my skin, let the sudden chill push me back to work.

I find a list of my mom's fears:

Poor health

Loneliness

Angry feelings

Fear of daughters not loving me

Depression

Always friendless

Getting old—older looking

Clutter—mail disorganization

Cats

Ants

I find her copy of Rilke's *Letters to a Young Poet* and open to a page she has marked: "We have no reason to mistrust our world, for it is not against us. Has it terrors, they are our terrors; has it abysses, those abysses belong to us; are dangers at hand, we must try to love them."

I find a scrap of paper that says "TAP WATER BURNED LIPS 10/17/09" next to a nearly empty glass.

I find a letter dated November 20 to an Oceanside police officer who had apparently visited her house: "I was taken aback by your title but assume you can see I am not a psychotic Oceanside resident," she had written. Later in the letter, she accused Dad's "cyber goons" of wiping out her computer and stealing files relating to the documentary she was producing, *The Art of Misdiagnosis.* I wonder what the officer's title was, wonder why he hadn't recognized her as psychotic—according to the letter, he had suggested she get a restraining order against my dad. If that officer had brought her in on an involuntary psychiatric hold, where would she, where would we, be today?

I find a red cloth-bound journal with a handwritten title page inside, "A Wife (in name only) by Arlene Baylen Brandeis," followed by a few poems, like "invisible mom":

adult daughter
walks past me
to lavish love and
affection upon
her father
don't you know?
i'm the one
whose
starving

Most of the journal is blank, but waves of guilt waft toward me from every page. I feel even more guilty when I realize I want to correct her misspellings, change "whose" to "who's," add some punctuation. *You criticize me even when I'm dead,* I can hear her say.

I find a shopping list with the word "Life" on it. She meant the cereal, a staple in her house, but the word looks so poignant, her desire for Life. The last word she ever said to me.

I find a letter she had written but never sent to me and Elizabeth in 2005, when she thought she was dying of heart valve disease. Part of it says "I think I have slightly more than a year to live. Oct '06, is the time I will pass into the next phase. Celebrate my life. I did it my way, and have no regrets. I hope the two of you and Dad also have no regrets." It closes with "I know you'll both keep my memory alive with your precious children. I will be a good spirit for all of you." I find myself wishing that this was her real last letter, her true final words. I wish I could imagine her as a good spirit.

I also find a handwritten will from her own mother inside a brittle envelope. In it, she bequeaths the family house on Mozart St. to my mom, Rochelle, and Don, "as you need a Home + you three are all ill + have to shift for yourselves." I wonder what illness she was referring to regarding my mom. Rochelle and their brother, Don, were both mentally ill. Did she know my mom was, as well, or was this related to the rheumatic fever—or at least what was called rheumatic fever—that plagued my mom when she was young? My grandmother also wrote that she hoped her seven other children would understand and that there should be "know hard feelings." I keep looking at that phrase, which repeats three times in the will, same spelling—"know hard feelings." That's what I want to let myself do now—know hard feelings. Face them and know them head on. Something that's never been easy for me.

And maybe it is my desire to know hard feelings that leads me to open the brown paper bag from the coroner's office—the large grocery sack folded over and stapled shut like a school lunch for a giant—that contains the clothes my mom was wearing when she killed herself. I've felt so removed from the physicality of her death. Every night, just as I'm about to fall asleep, images barge into my head of her hanging herself—the wrap, the drop; sounds barge into my head, too, the different gasps and gurgles that might have issued from her throat, but these are phantom imaginings, not the visceral reality of her suicide. I appreciate how everyone wanted to protect me in my postpartum state, but part of me wishes I could have seen her body in the mortuary, wishes I could have gone to the coroner's office to retrieve her things. This I can do, right here, right now. I can touch the clothes my mother died in.

Everything is bunched up inside the bag as if it had been ripped off her body without any care, and this makes it worse, knowing her body was treated roughly, no tenderness in the undressing.

My hands shake as I pull out one item after another:

- A black, white, and gray bouclé jacket with large black buttons.
- The red ribbed short-sleeved turtleneck she wore in her senior modeling photo, wrenched inside out.
- Black Chico's pants, also inside out, smelling of urine.
- White panties, inside out, too, smelling even more strongly of urine. I learn later that when someone hangs, their bladder lets loose.
- Tan and brown tiger-striped bra; this touches me, somehow, this touch of wildness she carried beneath her clothes.
- Ryka sneakers, white with silver trim, the lining bunched up inside as if her feet had been yanked out, smelling of sweat.
- Elizabeth's tan and black batik scarf, the one our mom had draped on her head the last night we saw her. Is this what she used to take her life?

I touch each piece of clothing gently and weep, laying them out on the floor around me the way I would lay out baby clothes when I was pregnant, imagining the life that was going to fill them; now, though, I imagine my mom's life ebbing away inside the fabric. I try to sense any lingering traces of her aliveness here—perhaps a lingering trace of Joy, her signature fragrance—but all I smell is her death. I hadn't known to prepare myself for this, the smell of her death. The smell reminds me of when a baby raccoon had died under my house many years ago; it took a while to find the source, and the stench kept getting stronger and stronger. But that was a dead animal, I tell myself, until I realize that's exactly what she was, too; in the hours between her death and the time she was found, she had already started to decay. I quickly stuff everything back into the bag, stomach heaving, the smell of her body burned into my brain.

2014

Dear Mom,

My therapist suggested I write to you. She thought it might help me find some clarity, help me understand how I am feeling about everything. It's good advice—I often don't know what I know until I write it down.

I wish I knew where to begin.

I suppose I could just write

WHY?

in giant letters smack in the middle of the page and leave it at that. I could be more specific: "Why did you kill yourself?" But even that would be too easy. Besides, I have too many other questions. Questions about our family's relationship with illness. Questions about our family's relationship with silence. Questions about your own relationship with your family. Questions, questions, so very many questions. Questions you'll never be able to answer.

It's always been hard to talk to you.

You gave me and Elizabeth an idyllic childhood in so many ways— I'll forever be grateful for the freedom we had to play and create and explore, for the family vacations we took to places like Disney World and Washington, DC, for the way you exposed us to museums and concerts and good food, the way you drove us to figure skating and dance classes, the way you made us feel our possibilities were limitless. Once I hit thirteen, things fell apart, but I had a practically perfect childhood. Still, even then, I didn't know how to talk to you.

I do know when that started. I was five years old. You had just eased your brown Chevy Impala into our spot in the communal parking garage under our apartment building in Evanston, Illinois, the spot you could glide straight into once the metal door clanked up on its track. The best spot, and it was ours. I suspected this made us the royalty of the building; I felt sad for all the other residents who had to back into tight spaces hemmed in by concrete pillars. You cultivated that feeling in us from the start—the sense that we were special, royal.

The garage was cool and smelled of leaded gasoline when I opened the back door; I took a deep breath, the scent as delicious to me as bread, and tried not to pay attention as you quietly got more and more upset. I wish I could remember what I had said to you; I remember everything from this moment except the words that set you off. They couldn't have been too bad—I was always careful with my speech—but you yanked the green and white Wieboldt's shopping bag off the floorboards, plucked Elizabeth from her car seat, and tore toward the door that led to the elevator.

"You never say anything unless it's something mean about me," you snarled. You had never spoken to me like that before. You had never said anything to indicate this is how you saw me: a girl who didn't speak except to cut you down. I thought I had always been your special flower, your good, smart girl, but now I knew you had been harboring a secret grudge against me. Now I knew you saw me as the enemy.

I trailed behind you and felt something slide shut across the inside of my throat, heavy as a manhole cover. It took me years to pry it back open, years before I could speak freely again. Not that I ever could around you; I wanted to, Mom, I really did, but something shut down inside me when you were around, some vital gleaming part.

I think of Gaston Bachelard: "What is the source of our first suffering? It lies in the fact that we hesitated to speak. It was born the moment we accumulated silent things within us." That moment in the garage was my moment, the moment I started to accumulate silent things. So many are still hoarded inside me, packed against my rib cage, settled in my gut.

It occurs to me now how strange it is that I felt silenced by you in a parking garage and you silenced yourself in a parking garage almost four decades later. Both of us in the bowels of apartment buildings, cutting words from our throats. I still have breath in my lungs—a gift I don't want to squander, a gift you tossed away—but sometimes I can feel the weight of that manhole cover clank back into place. Maybe writing this letter will help remove it for good.

My mom leaves a voice mail that makes my belly contract. The baby isn't due for a few more weeks, but I can picture him shooting out of me now like a cannonball.

"I don't know why you won't help me during the most difficult time of my life." Her voice quavers several octaves higher than normal. "I ask you to write one simple log line for Sundance and you won't do it. You're the writer; I'm not."

I take a deep breath and the scent of cat pee rushes in from the laundry room. The smell has plagued us since my new husband, Michael, and I moved to this little midcentury ranch house in Redlands, California, last month; we haven't been able to get rid of it, even after we ripped up the linoleum with our landlord's blessing and doused the floor boards with vinegar. But the office has French doors leading to a deep back yard, and the living room came with a piano, and the bathroom has vintage sky blue tile, and I'm going to give birth here—it's hard to not be fond of a house where one's going to give birth. And, truth be told, I'm starting to get used to the smell—it doesn't make my eyes water anymore, doesn't make me gag. Amazing what we can get used to, what we can learn to live with.

I call my mom back, but there's no answer, a relief; it's easier to deal with her over e-mail. I resend the log line I had written and shared with her last week, a fact she has forgotten, so ready to believe I'm part of a plot against her.

The Art of Misdiagnosis explores the abstract paintings of 70-year-old Arlene Brandeis, and how her art reveals not only her family history, but a larger story of medical ignorance and malpractice. The film features interviews with the Oceanside, CA, artist and her family as well as experts on the subjects of Ehlers-Danlos Syndrome and Porphyria, two disorders that have wracked the artist's family and are largely under- and mis-diagnosed in the general population. Brandeis sees herself as a medical advocate and wants this film to ultimately change emergency room procedure and doctor/patient communication in order to save lives that would otherwise be lost through misdiagnosis.

I have to admit, there are moments I let myself believe her propaganda, propaganda I helped her write. I know this documentary isn't going to get into Sundance; it's not going to change emergency-room procedure, either—it is more about her own paintings and her wild conjectures about our family's medical history than it is about changing the health care industry—but somehow when I wrote this log line, I let myself believe she could make a difference. Maybe because she has, in the past. She can be persuasive when she isn't delusional; sometimes even when she is. She spearheaded letter writing campaigns that removed guns and ammunition from the shelves of our local Kmart; she lobbied Congress to change divorce law.

The Art of Misdiagnosis has become my mom's magnum opus, her albatross. The project has brought her to the breaking point and has dragged me and my sister right to that edge, too. Elizabeth and I had asked our mom not to talk about our own journeys with illness in the film, but when she showed us the rough cut, there she was, talking at length about how her poor daughters had been misdiagnosed. She doesn't say anything about how both of us had fabricated our own illnesses, at least in part—we've tried to tell her this over the years, but she hasn't been able to hear it. She doesn't want anything to disrupt her own storyline, the story of herself as the heroic crusader, the warrior martyr of a mother who stood up to the big bad medical establishment and saved her blameless girls.

The mockup of her DVD cover features a photo of her perched at one end of a chaise lounge, legs crossed, her weight tilted onto her right hip. Her hair is dark and close cropped, a touch of white at the temples; she wears a mustard-colored jacket over a black turtleneck and black slacks, her fingernails cherry red. It looks as if she's either holding in a laugh or smirking, her lips pressed into a tight smile. Behind her hangs the triptych she painted, three large abstract canvases collectively titled "The Art of Misdiagnosis." The one on the left, *It Was Not Rheumatic Fever*, references her own childhood illness; the one in the middle, *It Was Not Crohn's Disease*, references me; the one on the right, *It Was Not an Eating Disorder*, references my sister. Three canvases full of geometric shapes she had blocked off with tape, then painted in muddied jewel tones. Three paintings that look like they should be hanging in the lobby of a Holiday Inn but somehow are supposed to represent medical injustice.

I want to drive the hour and a half south to her house in Oceanside and rip the paintings to shreds. I want to send an explosive through the back of each canvas, the way the resident director of my dorm detonated a cherry bomb through the painting of a naked woman he had asked me to hold out in front of my chest, the unexpected bomb scorching a hole straight through her belly. I wasn't hurt, but the speech he had spouted, pre-explosion, about innocence cut into me as if he had known I wasn't as innocent as I appeared, as if he had known something dark was hidden inside my own gut. He was fired shortly afterward, but not because I said anything. I won't say anything to my mom, either, won't do anything, now that she's almost done with the film. I'll bite my tongue, as I always do. I'll keep my hands to myself. I'll even help her with this project, this noble, misguided project, this project that perpetuates some of my biggest lies.

The ART of MISDIAGNOSIS

...The ... Genetic History of the Artist

A portion of all DVD sales will be donated to support medical research

An 8 page booklet is included with this DVD. It may help your doctor correctly diagnose you, your friends and family.

Expanded version

My mission is to empower and educate
those of us and our loved ones
whose conditions are not easily
diagnosed and sometimes
misdiagnosed by the medical community.

Making links for the little
known conditions
of Ehlers-Danlos Syndrome (EDS)
and joint problems,
cardiovascular problems,
even Sudden Cardiac Death with
Vascular Ehlers-Danlos Syndrome.

Making links from the
Acute Porphyrias and EDS
to Inflammatory Bowel Disease.

The links to undiagnosed
Acute Porphyrias and misdiagnosed

mental illness may be greater
than any of us realize.

There may be simple things
to do, to treat these conditions
when correctly diagnosed.

. . .

I would like to save others
from the pain,
loss and frustration my family
endured from the misdiagnosis
of these conditions.

This film and my artwork were inspired
by my own family experiences.

Arlene Baylen Brandeis
Artist/Executive Producer

[Camera pans over close ups of abstract paintings: *The Art of Misdiagnosis, Death and Transfiguration, Paternal DNA, Rochelle's Rhapsody*]

ARLENE BAYLEN BRANDEIS (Voice-over): I fully feel that
the spirits of my family have propelled me to do this
documentary, to tell this story, to try to educate
doctors, emergency rooms, nurses, the lay public. I
mean, this is my mission in making this documentary. I
think it has the potential to save lives and to stop a
lot of the misdiagnoses that go on in this country and
around the world.

Mom,

I keep thinking about your "scenarios," the stories you used to make up about people around us, the stories that delighted and troubled and sometimes scandalized me. I remember a particular one at Sam and Hy's Deli in Skokie when I was ten.

"You see that guy over there?" You pointed your bagel toward a portly man a few booths away. "That girl he's with? She's not his daughter."

I tried not to be obvious as I looked over at the girl at his table. She was probably around fourteen, a few years older than me, with dirty-blond hair, a smattering of pimples on her chin, dark makeup around her eyes. The girl reached into the stainless steel vat of complimentary pickles that sat on every table, using her fingers, not the metal tongs. Sam and Hy's Deli made the best new pick-les—crisp and bright green, still tasting of cucumber. I shuddered a little, imagining strangers sticking their hands in our own vat.

"Who is she?" Elizabeth asked, her mouth full of kreplach from her bowl of mish mosh soup.

"She's a runaway," you said, a devilish glint in your eye. "She was hitchhiking in Schaumburg when he picked her up. He's far enough from home that no one will recognize him here. He thinks if he buys her enough chocolate phosphates, he can have his way with her."

I wasn't sure what that meant exactly, but I felt a shiver of embarrassment, a sizzle of thrill, as I watched the girl eat her pickle. Would she give in to the sweaty man, pink as pastrami across the table from her? Or would she take the chocolate phosphates and run?

You did this at almost every restaurant. Over shrimp and lobster sauce at ChiAm in Chinatown or snappy Chicago-style hot dogs at

Fluky's, you would point to a table and tell us the diners' stories—
who was angry at who, who was betraying who, who had the most
horrible disease. You were utterly convincing. If the people themselves ever were to come up to our table and told us about their
lives, I doubt I would have believed them. It was your stories—your
"scenarios," as you called them—that carried the weight of truth.

Years later, when you started to accuse Dad of all sorts of crim-
inal behavior, it was hard to know at first if you had lapsed into
mental illness or if this was just another one of your scenarios, an
elaborate story built from the barest of evidence.

Joan Didion says we look for the sermon in the suicide. I'm not
sure I'm looking for a sermon. I'm just looking for you. I am aching to understand you now, to figure out your story, the path that
led to your unraveling. All I can really do is patch together a narrative from the spottiest of clues—the fragments you handed me, the
shards I can gather on my own. All I can really do is write my own
scenario, my own (mis)diagnosis of your life.

NOVEMBER 16, 2009

Thirty-seven weeks pregnant and I can't seem to stop crying. This is unusual for me. I tend to be an optimistic person. Relentlessly so. Probably obnoxiously so. I tend to be not just a glass-half-full kind of person, but a person who may just point out that the rest of the glass is filled with sunlight; an everything's-going-to-be-okay, go-with-the-flow, isn't-life-amazing type of person—in the world, at least, if not always in my own head.

Part of the reason my first marriage fell apart two years ago was because I didn't know how to let my husband know when I was upset. I spent way too much time smiling when I should have been honest with him. I kept so much frustration and anger pent up inside, so many silent things accumulating until they turned toxic under my skin. I've told myself I won't make the same mistake with my new marriage, and it appears my body is holding me to that, at least for now. My habitual smile is starting to fracture; whatever has been hiding behind it is seeping out.

Half the time, I have no idea why I'm crying. I cry at the midwife's office; I cry at our childbirth class. I cry when I learn on Facebook that my nineteen-year-old son, who lives with his dad, was hit by a car as he was riding his bike. He's okay, it seems, just banged up a bit, but that's not the kind of news a mom likes to stumble upon on social media, even when she isn't deeply hormonal. I cry when I get scared I've forgotten how to be a mother. It was so easy and joyful when my kids were babies, when they were young, when I created creativity festivals for their preschools, when we made "color meals" together—red bread with green butter, pasta with creamy blue sauce—when we curled up together with books and crayons and silly songs, when we crawled on the grass together to peer at ladybugs and worms. Now my kids are both teenagers—my daughter is almost sixteen—and parental instincts seem to have fled my body.

18

I always told myself I would be a mom whose kids could tell her anything, but I fear my kids have as much trouble talking to me as I do with my own mom. I love them both with all my heart and worry I've taken a wrong turn somewhere, maybe by smiling too much, by not acknowledging hard things enough, by not modeling how to be real.

I get another voice mail from my mom, this one saying she is driving to my house, saying she is going to spend the night. I leave a panicked voice mail on her phone, telling her it isn't the right time; I have grading to do—my Antioch MFA students have just turned in their work and I want to get to it before my UCLA Writers' Program students turn in their work, want to get to it before the baby comes, which feels like it could be any minute now.

"There's no place for you to sleep," I tell her voice mail, belly contracting again. Hannah's been using her bed as a desk and has been sleeping on the couch.

My mom calls back. She's turned around; she's on her way home. I am flooded with relief. Relief tinged with guilt, but relief all the same. There's no way I could have gotten work done with her there, wanting my attention. She gets offended if I so much as glance at a newspaper when she's in the same room; if I read my students' fiction in her presence, she'll find some way to make me feel horrible about it. Likely by inventing some medical emergency. Or telling me about my father's latest supposed acts of betrayal.

The doorbell rings around 10 p.m. Hannah, camped out on the vintage leopard print sofa, answers it. "Oh, hi, Nana," I hear her say, and my heart drops to the floor. I walk out of the office, bleary eyed from critiquing fiction. One of my students is writing a novel where a woman and baby die in childbirth and hang around their apartment as ghosts; another student is writing a novel in which a woman suffers horrific pregnancy complications during the Holocaust. Amazing novels, but not the most uplifting of pregnancy reading. *This is reality,* I tell myself as I read scenes of blood and rot, the baby twisting inside me—*it's good to be in touch with every aspect of reality.* When I was pregnant with Arin, I avoided all the pages about C-sections in my childbirth preparation book, and I ended up getting sliced open. Sometimes we're thrown face to face with the very things we're trying to avoid. Like my mom, here in my living room. She has a long cushion from an outdoor chaise lounge tucked under her arm. A few ties dangle down from the sides, like tiny insect legs on a huge thorax.

"I can sleep on this." She pushes past me and lays the cushion on the floor of my office, right behind my desk chair. When she looks up at me, she says, "You look awful."

"Thanks," I tell her. "I was just about to head to bed."

"Okay," she says, disappointed. There's clearly so much she wants to tell me, epic tales of her latest persecution. She's probably been repeating them to herself the whole seventy-five-mile drive from Oceanside. All she can get in, though, is "There's something wrong with my furnace" before I give her a cursory hug and close myself up in my bedroom. I hate to leave my husband and daughter to deal with my mom, but I am in no state to handle her. I may be able to face painful realities in my students' novels—in my own novels, even—but my own life is another story entirely. I lie down and my belly collects itself into a tight knot and the tears stream freely yet again.

When I get up in the morning, as late as I possibly can, my mom is calmer; I am less afraid of her. Michael has already left for work. Two mugs sit on the kitchen counter, encrusted with remnants of hot cereal; my mom's clearly held grits, Michael's cream of wheat. It touches me to think of them sharing this simple, pale breakfast. My mom has loved grits ever since we had them for the first time in Colonial Williamsburg when I was eight. She always buys boxes full of the instant packets to give to my sister, who can't get them in

Canada. She buys them for me, too, even though I can find them at any grocery store.

"We didn't have a meal together," she says, almost mournfully, as if this had been our last chance to break bread. "It feels funny to be here and not have a meal together."

"Yeah," I agree, hesitant to say anything else. When I get near her, words harden in my throat, get stuck there, like the grits I'll have to clean out of the mug later, stubborn as crystals in a geode.

Her face is softer this morning, more open. In fact, she seems to be pouring love and compassion toward me out of her eyes. It makes me flinch.

"I really have a lot of work to do today," I tell her and she looks predictably betrayed.

"I was thinking of going to my spiritual class, anyway," she says, her features closing themselves off again. She attends classes given by Nancy Tappe, a woman who developed the concept of "Indigo Children" and has written such books as *Understanding Your Life Through Color* and *Get the Message: What Your Car is Trying to Tell You*. The latter talks about how cars are mirrors of our own "internal warning system," what happens in our Hondas supposedly a metaphor for what's happening in our souls. My own internal warning system is beeping now, red lights clanging inside me. *Get her out, get her out, get her out now.*

I call Michael as soon as my mom and her cushion leave. Hannah's still asleep on the couch; once again, I haven't been able to get her up for school. A truancy officer who goes by Sergeant Hammer came to the house a couple of weeks ago and threatened her with "Hammer Time"; she was freaked out when he was standing in our living room, but now she sees him as a joke. (And, really, how could she not?) She's gone to class maybe a dozen times this semester; most of the time she's here, sleeping during the day, on her computer all night. I console myself by telling myself it could be a lot worse: she could be running away, shooting up, getting pregnant. At least I know where she is.

"What happened after I went to bed?" I whisper into the phone.

I can hear him sigh. "She had me check her laptop for bugs," he says. This doesn't seem so unusual at first. Part of his job is to check the computer system at UC Riverside for bugs; friends and family often use him as a free IT guy. But it soon becomes clear he means microphones, tracking devices, not computer viruses. "She keeps seeing pop.sbcglobal.yahoo.com inside her e-mail, and she thinks it's your dad hacking in. Pop, Papa." "Papa" is what my dad's grandkids call him, what I've taken to calling him, too, although my sister still calls him "Daddy." "She didn't believe me when I said it was the name of the server."

She had other complaints: the computer in the clubhouse of her complex was not secure; my dad somehow got his name onto her Internet account (Cox Communications denied this when she called); the producers she had hired from the local public television station were dropping *The Art of Misdiagnosis* from their slate. She showed Michael the e-mail in question; all he saw was an exchange where she had accused them of dropping the project and they had replied by saying they had no idea what she was talking about.

In the morning, her accusations had become worse. She told Michael she was being drugged in her house, that she would fall asleep in weird places and wake up feeling disoriented and dizzy. She told him that she saw someone in the house next door walking around a dark room with a flashlight, sure he was spying on her. When she called the neighbor, he told her he was looking for a cricket, but she didn't believe him. She thought her neighbor on the other side had been drilling through her floor to pump gas into her home. She thought the furnace was spewing gas.

No wonder she didn't want to sleep there.

"What should we do?" I ask, queasy. Her delusions haven't been this bad in years, if ever.

"The main thing you need to do right now is take care of yourself," he says. "You're sure she's gone?"

"She went to her class in Carlsbad." I try to take a deep breath, but my lungs are squashed by my enormous belly.

"Good," he says. "Don't let her come back."

Mom,

I guess we need to go back to the beginning—all the way back to birth.

The story of your psychosis begins and ends with birth.

Not your own birth at Chicago's Norwegian American Hospital in 1939, where you were the youngest of ten kids born to Gertrude and Benjamin Baylen—only the last two born in a hospital, where your mom was happy to be knocked unconscious.

Not my birth at Chicago's Michael Reese Hospital in 1968, when new mothers were fed steak and lobster dinners with champagne, the same hospital where Dad was born in 1919. You used to say you would rather give birth than go to the dentist; you were so lucky to have just a four-hour labor with me, a two-hour labor with Elizabeth four years later. You even had an orgasm pushing me out into the world; as uncomfortable as it was to hear you say "orgasm," I liked knowing this, liked knowing I was born in a rush of ecstasy, until I realized this set me up to disappoint you the rest of your life.

No—your psychosis was framed, strangely enough, by my giving birth.

Not the first time, in 1990, when my midwife laid me in the back of her van like a roll of carpet and whisked me to the hospital after she couldn't find the baby's heartbeat. I was twenty-two, had learned I was pregnant while I was in Bali for my study abroad my final semester of college. You weren't surprised when I called to tell you the news—your sister, Rochelle, the one who couldn't care for herself, the one who still lived in your childhood house with your equally low-functioning brother, Don, had dreamed I was pregnant the night before. You were still living in the Chicago area, two thousand miles away from Riverside, California; you fainted in the bathroom when you learned about the hospital transfer, knocking Dad over, pinning him against the tub.

It killed you to not be in the hospital with me. We spent a lot of time together in hospitals, the two of us.

It turned out the cord had been wrapped around the baby's head three times, then once under his arm and around his neck again, leading to an emergency C-section.

Hard not to think of you now. Cords. Necks.

You never forgave me for asking you to wait two weeks to come meet your first grandchild; this had been recommended by our childbirth instructor, who said it was good to give new parents time to bond with the baby before having out of town visitors. You were so jealous of Matt's parents, who lived in Southern California and got to meet Arin his first day in the world. My father-in-law had photos developed at a one-hour place and sent them to you overnight, but that was no substitute for holding the baby in your arms.

Three years later, you booked a flight as soon as you heard I had given birth to Hannah. "You're not making me wait two weeks this time," you warned. You showed up without Dad, which seemed weird. Things only got weirder from there.

NOVEMBER 21, 2009

Aside from a few frenzied phone calls, my mom leaves me alone the rest of the week. I start to feel as if I can breathe more freely, as if I can focus on work, as if I'm not in anyone's crosshairs. And then the doorbell rings late Saturday afternoon.

"Oh, hi, Nana," I hear Hannah say, and I feel as if I've fallen into a bad recurring dream. I walk out from the office to find my mom, chaise lounge cushion once again in tow. This time, she looks even more agitated. She is shaking, hyperventilating. Her voice is high pitched, hysterical—I can't even tell what she's saying, she's speaking so fast. Hannah slips away and locks herself in her room. I wish I could join her.

"Mom," I start. "Are you okay?"

"Of course I'm not okay!" she shrieks, lunging toward me. "What do you think? This is the most difficult time of my life!" A sentence she likes to repeat; she gloms on to certain sentences and plays them like a DJ sample.

Michael steps between us with his lanky body, his mop of light brown curls. "Why don't we go for a walk?" he tells her, and ushers her back outside. He looks over his shoulder at me and I mouth a silent "Thank you."

As soon as the door closes behind them, I try to reach my sister. I call her cell and home number numerous times. I leave several text messages—"SOS," "Help!," "Mom is the worst I've ever seen her!"—and she doesn't respond. Elizabeth is a midwife in Toronto; maybe she's at a birth. She's scheduled to fly out next week to assist me in labor. I finally call her fifteen-year-old daughter and ask if she knows how to reach her mom's pager. Once I punch in that number, Elizabeth calls back right away. She's at a party. I can hear music and chatter in the background. It feels disorienting to know people are having fun when I'm stuck inside a horror movie.

"I don't know what to do!" My voice is almost as hysterical as our mom's had been. "What should I do?"

"Take a deep breath," she tells me, her voice immediately soothing over the phone. She sounds concerned, but not overly so; she sounds as if she's had some wine. I start to wonder if I'm overreacting. "Don't let her rattle you, sweetie," she says. "And keep me posted. I love you and that baby so much."

I take some deep breaths. I tell myself to detach, to let go. To not clench myself in fear. It will be okay, I tell myself; it will be okay. When I touch my belly, the baby pushes back, as if in reassurance.

By the time my mom and Michael return, I'm feeling less doomed. My mom looks more subdued, herself, although Michael looks shaken.

"We need to find her a safe house," he says.

"A safe house?" I whisper after my mom closes herself in the bathroom.

"She's in bad shape," he whispers back, "and she thinks she's being abused. If she goes to a safe house, maybe someone will figure out what's really going on and she can get the help she needs."

"Brilliant." I give him a kiss, then start to research safe houses online.

My mom comes into the office and tosses a printout on my desk. It's the Diagnosis column from the *New York Times*, one from late last month, with the title "Perplexing Pain."

"Your father is behind this." She leans against the doorway, chin raised, like some thug in a '50s movie.

If my dad could pull strings with the *New York Times*, I want to tell her, I would have been reviewed by them by now. Instead, I just say, "What do you mean?"

"Look at the name of her book." I flip to the bio on the last page; the italicized print reads "*Lisa Sanders is the author of 'Every Patient Tells a Story: Medical Mysteries and the Art of Diagnosis.'*"

"How could Dad possibly be behind this?" I ask.

"He gave her my title," she says, her voice edging higher. "*The Art of Diagnosis, The Art of Misdiagnosis.* You think that's a coincidence?!"

"Mom." I try to keep my voice calm. "You know how slow the publishing industry is. Books take a year to be published, sometimes more. She had the title long before you did."

"Titles can be changed in an instant," my mom said. "And look—this is all about porphyria!"

Now this is unfortunate. Porphyria is one of the two diseases my mom highlights in *The Art of Misdiagnosis.* One of the two diseases she feels a proprietary claim over; she had wanted to be porphyria's herald, the one to usher it into the public eye.

I had a borderline positive test for porphyria when I was nineteen. After feeling pretty good for a few years following an early teenage illness, I was beset by occasional but intense stomach pain my first semester at college. A doctor asked my mom whether we had looked into the possibility of porphyria—she glommed on to this and dragged me to a hospital in Connecticut that specialized in the metabolic disorder during my summer break.

I found porphyria quite intriguing—the name come from *porphyra,* which means "purple pigment," my favorite color, and the illness is responsible for all sorts of strange phenomena: purple pee, vampirism, werewolfism, the madness of King George. My stomach pains were tame as far as porphyria symptoms went, but perhaps some of the weirdness would rub off on me. At the very least, it would be a cool disease to tell people about, much less embarrassing than the Crohn's disease I had been diagnosed with a few years earlier. The tests at the hospital weren't conclusive, but the borderline positive was enough for my mom; she grabbed onto the diagnosis and ran with it, and I accepted it by default. I accepted the fact that I should eat a high carbohydrate diet (the main way to manage porphyria), that I should avoid certain medications, that this was the illness that defined me now.

I don't remember much about the trip, just that everyone at the hospital was extra solicitous. My mom had taken it upon herself to circulate an article about me to all the doctors and nurses on my team; it was about me being named a "Steward of Liberty for the next 100 years" the previous fall, when one of my essays had been installed in the centennial time capsule of the Statue of Liberty. My essay was about the human spirit; it rhapsodized about how even if someone is imprisoned, their imagination can always run free.

"I want them to know who you are," my mom said. "They're not going to call you crazy here."

Of course I couldn't tell the doctors my real story, especially not once they started treating me like a famous writer. I hadn't told anyone my real story yet, although my doctors in Chicago had guessed at it, and my mom had accused them of malpractice as a result. Some steward of liberty I was—not even free enough to share my own truth.

I try to read the *Times* article, but my eyes keep returning to the title: "Perplexing Pain." Perfect words for this moment.

"Your dad is behind this," she says again. "He wants to steal my thunder. He wants everyone to know about porphyria so my movie will be moot!"

Over the years, I've been tested for porphyria again—tests where I had to gather twenty-four hours' worth of urine in a big brown jug that sat in a tub of ice in the corner of the bathroom—and it's always come back negative. My mom insisted these tests were notoriously inaccurate. She finally paid for me to have an expensive new blood test, a test that was supposed to be much more precise and definitive—it came back negative, too. Porphyria: yet another misdiagnosis. My mom refused to believe this. She thought I was lying. She even called my doctor; when he confirmed it, she didn't believe him, either. She thought my dad had paid him off.

I was a bit sad to let go of the porphyria diagnosis; it seemed to explain so much. Porphyria could be triggered by hormonal changes—I had imagined that's why I had gotten sick when I neared puberty; that's why I had gotten sick when I took birth control pills in college; that could be why my mom's delusions started around the time she hit menopause. Porphyria can cause "intermittent psychotic episodes"—it says so right on the back of her DVD cover. Without porphyria, the answers are not so simple.

"Mom," I say, "sometimes there are just coincidences. Remember when I was writing *Self Storage* and I found out Michael Cunningham had just published a novel based on *Leaves of Grass*?" I adore Michael Cunningham's work and worried my own Whitman-inspired novel would seem derivative, would never hold a candle to his. "Or when my working title for *Fruitflesh* was *Writing from the Body*, and a book called *Writing from the Body* came out just before I finished my first draft?"

My mom gives a hesitant nod.

"I was devastated both times, but then I realized there was still room for my projects, my voice. There's still room for yours, too."

My mom actually seems to consider this. For a moment, she looks thoughtful; she looks more like her normal self. "There is the collective unconscious . . ." she starts, and it sounds so lucid, so intelligent, I start to hope she can pull out of this. Then her face clouds again. "But your father is working to get this woman a show on PBS! They'll never air my film now!"

"And you know this how?" I ask, heart deflating.

"Why do you never support me?" she cries. "You and your sister call yourselves feminists but you never support your own mother!"

"Mom." I slump back in my desk chair, all my energy suddenly gone. "What do you want me to say?"

"I want you to say you believe me!" she shouts.

"I'm sorry," I tell her. She lunges forward and for a moment, I fear she's going to strike me. My belly tightens protectively.

"I have to get out of here," she says, walking past me.

"You don't need to do that," I say, even though I want nothing more than for her to leave.

"Yes I do," she says, now in the doorway on the other side of the office. "I need to pick up some vitamins; I need to get something to eat. My blood sugar is through the roof." She gives me a look saying that if she goes into a diabetic coma, it will be all my fault.

Michael offers to take my mom on some errands; after they leave, I resume my search for safe houses in the area. My own house feels much safer without her in it. Hannah even ventures out of her room.

"Are you okay?" she asks. I nod and smile, grateful; she gives me a little hug and retreats to the kitchen.

None of the safe houses I call have any beds available, and when I explain my mom's situation, most of them tell me they are not the right place for her, anyway.

"We are here for women who need to get out of abusive situations," one operator tells me. "Your mom needs a hospital."

The problem is, she would never go to a hospital voluntarily. At least not for this. I'm starting to realize it's not fair to ask a safe house to do something I haven't had the guts to do myself over the last sixteen years—force her to get help. Every time my family has taken steps in that direction, it's blown up in our faces.

How can you get help for someone who doesn't think she needs it? What house is safe for someone whose brain has turned against itself?

When I hear the front door open, I brace myself, but Michael is alone.

"Where is she?" I ask when he walks into the office.

"She doesn't want you to know," he says.

"What does she think I could do to her?" I look down at my huge belly. I can barely get out of a chair.

"I took her to the Best Western in Loma Linda," he says, "but she was worried Middle Eastern men were watching her when she checked in."

"So she might come back?" I ask, feeling a wave of panic along with a wave of embarrassment over her recent fear of Middle Eastern men. I know it's related to her trip to Egypt three years ago, but it seems like a strange lapse of her normally progressive values.

"I don't think so," he says. "Her car is still here, and she's pretty mad at you."

I can't help it; I feel guilty. I wonder what I could have done, could have said differently. It always comes back to this: me beating myself up.

Michael tells me about their conversation on their walk and in the car. She had gone to my dad's house this morning to copy some things from his computer and return his cell phone, which she had borrowed. When he offered her a drink, she would only take a sealed one. He poisoned her anyway, she said; he sprayed her with some sort of device.

"She kept saying she needs to get away," he tells me. "She needs to escape. She can't believe Buzz followed her out here to California. She wants to get away from him." My dad moved here a few years after she did, after he finally retired from advertising at the age of eighty-five. He lives three miles from her in Oceanside. When she isn't having one of her episodes, they are best friends and see each other almost every day.

"She thinks if she finds a safe house, she'll have time to pull her evidence together," he says. "Time to make a case."

Her "evidence" will never make sense to anyone but herself. The notes she's thrown at me over the years don't incriminate anyone but her.

"She talked a lot about you and Elizabeth, too." He looks at me to gauge whether I want to hear this; I nod for him to go ahead. "She doesn't understand how she could have sacrificed everything for the two of you and you still don't believe her."

This isn't new information. I've heard it many times over. She said as much before she left. Still, somehow, it stings. I'm such a people pleaser, I even want to please my delusional mother. Someone who could never be pleased.

I think about our wedding, four months ago. My sister and I each eloped in the '90s, and our mom still holds a grudge. Her mother had died a month before her own wedding; how dare her daughters exclude her from theirs? This was unforgivable, a fact she reminded us of, often. Michael's and my wedding was a chance for me to redeem myself. She wanted to be involved, so I asked her to make some appetizers—a task she normally loved and excelled at; I asked her to walk me down the aisle with my dad, one of them on each arm, something a mother is not usually invited to do. I thought she would be thrilled, that this would be a dream come true. Instead, she spent the whole day complaining about the work I had forced her to do and saying she thought she was having congestive heart failure. Instead, she printed up an e-mail she had sent me, one I had ignored, one suggesting Michael's dad and his wife should sit at the head table with the bride and groom while Michael's mom, Jette, should sit across the room with her ex-husband's children from his current marriage. She left it where Michael's mom could find it, and Jette went into a tizzy, slapping the printed-out e-mail like a tambourine as she stormed around the reception hall.

Still, I look back on that day with great fondness. The marzipan pears on the cake. The vines embroidered on my dress. The way Michael and I kept kissing each other during the ceremony, leaning forward and kissing even before we were named spouses for life, our curly hair coiling together. Once, when I was still married to my first husband, a stranger came up to me and Michael and said, "If you two have kids, imagine the hair." It was something we couldn't have dared to dream about then, but here we were, getting married, a baby predisposed to curly hair growing in my belly. Kissing, kissing, kissing.

[BUZZ BRANDEIS, FORMER HUSBAND, sits in front of
the bougainvillea on the patio of ARLENE's house in
Oceanside.]

BUZZ: I had known Arlene thirty-six years. She had no
    interest in painting, had never shown any interest
    in painting, had never picked up a paintbrush to my
    knowledge, and then one day she said, "Buzz, I have to
    paint. I need to paint."

[ARLENE BAYLEN BRANDEIS stands in front of *Four Dead
Brothers*, yellow, green, and red paint dripping down the
canvas. The red paint forming an unintentional letter
"A" right next to her head. She is wearing a lime-green
jacket over a black turtleneck, a horizontal silver
pendant draped over the front of it, a small microphone
attached to her lapel. Her hair is cropped short; she is
wearing glasses and small hooped clip-on earrings (gold;
her ears will only accept gold. Her earlobes have a
permanent crease from years of gold clip-ons).]

ARLENE: Out of the blue, I just had this need, this urge,
    to make art, and I had been a docent for years; I
    loved contemporary art, I like to study it, I like
    giving tours at the museum. But all of a sudden, I
    had this welling up of need to make art and I thought
    I was going to paint about opera because I had been
    in operas, I had little walk-on parts at Lyric Opera
    of Chicago as a supernumerary and we had been opera
    subscribers for twenty-seven years so we saw a lot of
    opera and I was sure I was going to paint about opera,
    and I knew it was going to be geometric or I knew
    it was going to be drip painting, and I thought I'd

kind of play around with art posters in some kind of abstract way, and so I had this welling up of a need to make art.

BUZZ: And so she started trying to figure out how to do that.

ARLENE: I want to work large. My home, you know, just wasn't right for painting, so I found this little studio in Aurora, Illinois, which was about fifty miles west of Chicago, and it was above a store and it had windows to the south, that was perfect lighting, and it had this whole wall of windows and I was able to get a six-month lease.

And so I got into the studio and I bought all these canvases and some house paint and, later, acrylic paint and I thought, you know, what am I going to . . . where am I going to start? And then I started thinking about my sister and I thought, well, maybe it's not opera I need to start painting about; it's probably about my sister, Rochelle, and her sad life, and I started thinking of *Rhapsody in Blue*—I knew I was going to paint to music—and sure enough, all of the flood of memories . . . This was in the year 2000, and these deaths, of course, began with my mother in 1967, and so this was long after all of these five deaths, and it was like, it was like something otherworldly happened. There was a spirit· that embodied me and it was kind of automatic, like automatic writing that you hear some people talk about. For me, it was automatic painting, but I knew what it was when it was happening; I knew what it was about, and all of a sudden, just these paintings poured forth.

BUZZ: After a couple of weeks, I thought I'd visit her
and I was astonished by what I saw. She had started
to paint and was in the midst of painting a couple
of large pieces, and I couldn't believe what I saw—
they were colorful, the design was there, and it just
amazed me because she had no training at all.

Mom,

You oohed and ahhed over baby Hannah. You made a big show out of each toy, each piece of clothing, you brought for both grandkids, drawing each one slowly of out of a plastic Gap bag like a magician pulling a bunny from a hat. But something was off. Something in your eyes. In your restless energy. And then you started to talk about white vans.

"They're following me," you said. "White vans following me everywhere I go."

I flashed on when I was a kid and a girl in our area had been abducted into a white van with no back windows; I had grown up distrusting every single white cargo van.

"There are lots of white vans around here," Matt told you as I tried to tamp the panic rising up my spine.

"Yeah," I added. "Remember when we were in Scottsdale and the parking lot at our hotel was full of white cars?" It had looked eerie, like a ghostly car cult. Then someone explained to us that everyone had white cars to reflect away the Arizona sun. "It's like that."

"I have the license plate numbers." You glared at me.

You could be stubborn, narcissistic, judgmental, melodramatic, overly sensitive—when you weren't being creative, supportive, ballsy, generous, loving and fun—but you had never been paranoid before. This was new, and this was terrifying. I was grateful Arin was busy with his new puzzle and couldn't see the expression on your face. Or mine.

"Your father's behind it," you said. "Your father put them up to it."

"Mom, what are you talking about?" I asked, cold sheets of adrenalin cascading down my body. Dad was, is, the most gentle guy a person could imagine—soft spoken, funny, completely devoted to you, even now.

"There's a lot about your father you don't know," you said.

.   .   .   .

You showered me with papers. It was like they were rice or flower petals at a wedding. You tossed one white page after another, hurling them across the coffee table, but these pages weren't thrown in celebration; these pages were thrown with anger, with spite. You spit them at me like bullets while I held newborn Hannah; I wrapped myself around her so the pages wouldn't nick her new skin.

You told me the papers meant Dad was hiding millions of dollars from you, from us. You told us he was part of a vast international money laundering scheme, that these "hand notes"— random jottings of numbers—proved it.

"Look!" you yelled as you tossed another page, as I cowered, frozen, as if the paper had been laced with anesthesia. "Look what your father has done!"

The pages fell around me like snow. I was covered in a drift of white and numbers. Everything I knew was drifting away. I was still bleeding from birth, wild with sleep deprivation. Life was already a fog, but you turned it into a blur, a whirl, dizzying as those carnival rides that plaster riders to the wall. The only thing that kept me from spinning off my own axis was the sweet weight of the baby in my lap.

NOVEMBER 22, 2009

My belly wakes me like a punch at 6 a.m. This is no Braxton-Hicks contraction. I wait for another one, which arrives a few minutes later, making me gasp, then another, then another.

I'm having a baby.

I'm having a baby!

Up until now, the baby has felt somewhat theoretical. I've felt him move, of course; I've talked and sung to him; I've seen him on the ultrasound; I have blankets and diapers and onesies ready; my breasts are leaking colostrum, but part of me has believed I'd be pregnant forever. Part of me hasn't fully comprehended I'm going to have a real newborn in my life again after almost sixteen years. A rush of excitement travels through me. A baby!

I remember the whorl of hair on the back of Arin's head when he was a newborn; I remember the little rosebud purse of Hannah's lips, the way she held them in an "o" right after she was born, as if she was in constant amazement at the world she had just entered. I remember the burnt sugar smell of their new scalps, the way they looked right into my eyes as they nursed.

I should probably let Michael sleep—we have a big day ahead of us—but I can't help myself; I whisper, "I'm in labor," into his ear.

"Awesome." He touches my belly and gives me a groggy smile without opening his eyes.

Then I remember my Mom is right down the street and the excitement curdles in my veins.

"What if she shows up?" I ask. "I can't go through labor with my mom here!"

"Her car is here," he reminds me, his eyes still closed. He's snoring before I slip back out of bed. I'm glad. Michael is intensely empathic—if I get a headache, he gets a headache; if I get a urinary tract infection, he gets a urinary tract infection. If anyone has ever been a candidate for sympathetic pregnancy, it's Michael. I worry that I'll have to support him through labor more than he'll have to support me. Plus he often gets deeply tired—dark orange circles under his eyes kind of tired, skin-turning gray kind of tired, the kind of tired that makes me worry about his health, which makes me worry about our future. The more sleep he can get this morning, the better.

I sit on the giant pink ball in the office and call my sister. I groan with each contraction, and she coaches me through it, her voice calm and encouraging. Her clients are lucky to have her as a midwife.

"I wish I was there," she says. She's not due in until Thursday. Thanksgiving.

"I wish you were, too."

"I'll try to get an earlier flight," she promises.

Michael shuffles into the office a couple of hours later, his curly hair wild.

He checks his e-mail. "Huh," he says. "She went home."

"What?" I ask, the ball rolling beneath me. "How?"

He gestures for me to come over. When I do, he pulls me onto his lap even though I'm worried I'm going to crush his skinny legs. He nestles his chin on my shoulder as I read the e-mail:

Michael, you are the dearest son-in-law any woman could hope for. Thank you again. I hope both you and Gayle are feeling well, it is not my intent to create havoc in her life at this tender time. Unfortunately, someone else has created havoc in my life, the domino effect happens.

I left the hotel around 2:30 am. I knew it would not be a good night when I saw what I told you about. A noisy group occupied rooms 213 and 215, on either side of me. They were speaking loud and stomping around outside my room. It sounded like a couple, and at least two east Indian men, speaking on the cell phones asking more to join them. When they entered the rooms on either side of me, I dressed, asked for security and a cab. The night desk clerk came up and put me in the taxi to pick up my car. I did manage to sleep from about eight to midnight.

We will need to decide how to manage Thanksgiving. I am unable to be with Buzz. It would put me in a coma. Perhaps since Elizabeth is not due in till 2:30, and I will bring much of the food, Buzz could come late or wait until Friday. Another option would be for me to wait to see Elizabeth until Friday. I'll do whatever. The first Thanksgiving I was in California, Elizabeth was unsympathetic about my being alone. She said "you choose to be alone," because I moved to California. At the time I did not understand my separation was a package deal with my daughters. And both Gayle and Elizabeth never understood my leaving their father was not a choice but a need.

Thanks again.

The drive home was very foggy in spots, but I managed just fine.

Much love to all of you.
Your very appreciative mom-in-law

Reading my mom's words makes me wonder once again if I'm being too hard on her. Her love is coming through the e-mail in a way it hadn't in person. The fact that she understands this is a "tender time," that she doesn't want to cause havoc, softens my heart toward her. Maybe she's not as far gone as I had feared. Maybe she's just foggy in spots.

"She's not right down the street," Michael whispers into my ear. I nod as a contraction lifts me off his lap.

"Time to call the midwife?" he asks.

"I think so," I tell him, trying to breathe.

"I better set up the birthing tub," he says, and heads into our bedroom to deal with the folded up inflatable pool and the monstrous-looking air pump. It starts to whine in the background like a lawn blower, and I growl through another contraction. Hannah peeks out of her room to see what all the ruckus is about.

"I'm in labor," I tell her, still bent over, and she looks alarmed. She calls her dad, who she hasn't seen in weeks, and asks him to pick her up. I don't blame her. I know how hard it is to see one's own mother wild-eyed, strange sounds coming from her mouth.

From: Arlene Brandeis
To: gaylebrandeis@gmail.com
Cc: Elizabeth Brandeis
Sent: Friday, March 27, 2009 2:28pm
Subject: "The ART of MISDIAGNOSIS"

Dear Gayle and Elizabeth,

I want to let you know about the producers I met with, Kerry at KPBS and Peter at KOCT. They are both astonished (I'm unfortunately accustomed to being treated that way by both of you) by your lack of support. You may both want to reconsider, and decide to support me, and help with my project, with your presence and individual stories.

Having successful and powerful women who have transcended these genetic problems, is the face I want to present. The whole point, to give hope to others and to lift these two conditions out of the pack of 6000 conditions in NORD, National Organization of Rare Diseases. I fervently believe Porphyria and EDS are not rare conditions, only rarely diagnosed properly. Desirée Lyon told me something interesting. "Porphyria had a spike during the Atkins Diet craze." The importance of understanding the role of carbohydrates and vitamin C are such simple things for the general public to understand. There may be hundreds of thousands of others who are like Rochelle, lives that have been ruined by mental health professionals misdiagnosing many like her. I also believe there is a link to post-partum depression and Porphyria. There may also be thousands who could be saved from sudden death with vitamin C, from Vascular EDS.

Another reason your absence would reflect poorly on you, the program will be dedicated in the memory of your grandmother.

The producers both think this is an important project that could attract a lot of attention.

I want to be sure if we film the EDS group in my home on the 27 of April, you will not make me uncomfortable, Elizabeth, talking about my art and the medical history of my daughters. I may change the date of that shoot if you give me a hard time. There is a family (mother and two sons with EDS) who want to come in from Texas on that date. Cindy Lauren, the Executive Director of the Ehlers-Danlos National Foundation will also be in from LA. Dad will also record his impressions of my "painting out of the blue in 2000." At the very least, it would be good to have both of you help behind the scenes. We may also film a Porphyria expert on LA on May 6, with Desiree Lyon, Executive Director of the American Porphyria Foundation, who will also come in from out of state.

Love,
Mom

Mom,

So much of the time period after Hannah's birth is hazy to me. Did I confront you or was I was frozen, numbed by your flurry of paper? I am guessing the latter, but it would be good to know for sure.

I texted Matt to see if he could help me fill in some blanks, help illuminate some spans of that time that have gone dark in my brain. He texted back saying he wasn't interested in rehashing the past. Rehashing is all I am interested in, though—gathering choppy bits of my life, throwing them together, trying to create something cohesive; a bunch of leftovers seasoned to taste, like any good hash.

The first time Dad called you, he said, "I love hashed brown potatoes!" when you answered the phone.

No "Hello." No "Um, this is Buzz, we met the other night at the Quadrangle Club?" Just a bright, enthusiastic, "I love hashed brown potatoes!"

Fortunately—for the sake of my own, and our descendants', existence—you didn't hang up. Fortunately, you laughed. Fortunately, you remembered the line, which came from an Ionesco play you had both seen the night you met.

You had been taking a Great Books class through Adult Education at the University of Chicago; your class attended the play and a reception on campus afterward. Dad came as the guest of one of your classmates. He was getting over a rough divorce; he had been living in a small hotel room where he had to put bottles of milk on the window sill to keep them cold, where there wasn't much room for his teenage kids Sue and Jon to visit. You were getting over the death of Eli, the man you would consider your true love the rest of your life. Dad thought you looked exotic; he imagined you were Greek.

I can visualize that night more clearly than I can picture much of my own past. I can see your short beehive hairdo, your salmon-colored cocktail dress, the cigarette perched in your elegant hand; I can smell the waft of whiskey in the room, can see Dad's slicked-back hair, the gap between his front teeth, his fitted suit as he leans toward you, enchanted. He looks so young; you are surprised to learn he is twenty years older than you. I hear live piano music, ice clinking in glasses, people talking about absurdism as they lift rumaki from silver trays. I can see you trying to keep up with the conversation, smiling, using words you're not sure you fully understand.

Call me naive, but until you started to spout your accusations, I thought you and Dad had a perfect marriage. You laughed a lot together. You held hands in public. I never saw you argue. You complained about just about everyone else in your life, but you had never once complained about him to me. Your wedding anniversary was February 22, and on the twenty-second of every month, he gave you flowers and you gave him a card addressed to D.W.M.—Darling Wonderful Man. Neither of you had any real friends outside of each another; you were one another's world.

"It was an unusual love affair," Dad often says to this day; I put the emphasis on unusual now, but he still puts the emphasis on love.

Here's one thing I remember: the earthquake.

The Northridge earthquake hit when Hannah was twenty-five days old. You were still in town. As our tiny duplex in family student housing shook, blinds swaying in the windows like hula skirts, Matt and I scooped the kids from the mattress on the floor that was our family bed—Arin in Matt's arms, Hannah in mine—and stood in the doorway to ride it out. Both kids slept through the whole thing while Matt and I smiled nervously at each other over their heads.

You called from your hotel room after everything settled down.

"Someone was shaking my bed!" you yelled. You had never experienced an earthquake before, other than a gentle one that hit Chicago when I was a few months old and made my baby swing—my favorite place to hang out—wobble back and forth on its metal legs.

"It was an earthquake, Mom," I told you. "A big one. Turn on the news."

"I thought someone was under the bed." You were silent for a moment, then said, "This phone is bugged—we need to be careful."

"Mom," I started, but I didn't know what else to say.

After Northridge, there was a lot of talk about earthquake preparedness. Matt and I took heed and stocked the shed behind our house with bottled water and flashlight batteries and canned beans.

I don't know what I could have done to prepare for your psychosis.

Another thing I remember: you kept talking about Santa Barbara, how you wanted to get to Santa Barbara. It was unclear what exactly you hoped to find there, if there was something specific, or if you were just drawn to the place on the map—you were cagey when I asked; it just kept coming up: *Santa Barbara, Santa Barbara, I need to go to Santa Barbara.*

Hannah had her first post-birth checkup scheduled at our family doctor's office, so Matt and I asked if you could pick Arin up at preschool. We were hesitant to do this—we weren't that comfortable with you being alone with our son, but we weren't able to make other arrangements. We wouldn't be gone long, we reasoned. The preschool was just a couple of blocks away from our house; we left his car seat with you, but suggested you walk there and back with him instead. You'd always been a scary driver; I didn't believe in guardian angels (you thought your mother was yours), but I wasn't sure what else could explain how you hadn't gotten in a major crash with your distracted, erratic driving.

When we got back from the doctor's office, your car was gone. The house was empty, Arin's car seat just inside the front door. Wherever you had driven with him—if he even was with you—you had done so without his car seat.

This was before cell phones, of course. We had no way to get in touch with you, no way to find out where you were.

"Should we call the police?" I asked Matt.

"I think you need forty-eight hours to file a missing person report," he said.

"What if it's a kidnapping?" I asked. Just saying the word "kidnapping" wrenched a sob from my gut. I ached for Arin with every fiber of my being. I ached for him so intensely, I felt like my heart was going to burst through my chest, my throat, my eyeballs. I tried to visualize where you were, how he was. Were you on your way to Santa Barbara? Was he scared? Was he safe? Had you even buckled his seat belt?

We called the police. How could we not? They put someone on it and told us to call if you turned up.

Three hours later, you came breezing through the door with Arin and a bunch of Kmart bags, looking happy as can be, completely unaware we had been in a total panic. I scooped Arin into my arms and cried and cried, so relieved to see him again, to be able to smell his sweaty little boy head.

"Where were you?" Matt demanded, and you looked offended that he would talk to you in such a tone.

You held up the bags. "We went to Kmart," you said, as if this was the most normal thing in the world.

"For three fucking hours?!" Matt yelled, Hannah sleeping in his arms.

"There's a lot to see," you said.

"We thought you had gone to Santa Barbara," I said, still crying. Arin was crying in my arms at this point, too. I couldn't get enough of him, his pulse, his warmth, his solid little body—I wanted to fuse him against my chest. "We called the police."

"You did what?!" You were livid. "You want to lock me away just like your father!"

"You could have left a note," I told you. "We were terrified."

"I'm the one who should be terrified," you said. "If something happens to me, it's not suicide."

NOVEMBER 22, 2009

In our childbirth class, the instructor had us write an "ideal but realistic" birth story. In my story, my parents pick up Elizabeth at the airport on Thanksgiving day, the Hyundai full of stuffing and sweet potatoes and Tofurkey. After our meal, my mom and dad head back to Oceanside, and I start to go into labor; my sister and Michael and I take a walk to Gerard's, our local market, to help move things along. The cashier who thinks Michael looks like Jim Morrison asks if the baby is coming soon. We tell her I'm in labor and she says we better get to the hospital; when I say we are planning a home birth, she wishes us luck and hands me a stick of purple rock candy from the box by the register as a gift.

My mom's e-mail makes it clear we're not all going to have Thanksgiving together, but I can't worry about that right now. Pretty soon, the labor is intense enough, I can't worry about anything but getting through each contraction. Labor has a knack for burning everything away—the outside world, modesty, the manhole cover in my throat. I find myself able to say exactly what I want (my thighs squeezed, hard), exactly what I don't want (Michael getting in the birthing tub with me) without hesitation. It is a bit discomfiting to realize how radical and unfamiliar this feels.

Even with this clarity, though, I'm flailing. I thrash around in the water like a fish on a hook, sputtering and frantic, unable to find a comfortable place to rest. And I'm not progressing, even though the contractions are tearing me in half. In my "ideal but realistic" birth story, I am pretty calm except when I head into transition, but so much of this labor feels like transition; there isn't a span within it when I don't feel full of doubt, don't feel like my life is in danger.

. . . .

When Michael and I were instructed to come up with a peaceful image, an image we could focus on during labor, Michael suggested the picnic my mom had arranged for us on the beach in Oceanside a couple of months ago. She and my dad had lugged from her car a card table and chairs, a tablecloth, beautiful serving dishes full of pasta salad, arugula salad, fruit, cheese, and bread, along with salmon for herself and my dad, and set them up on the sand. We ate and watched the sun set over the water. It was an idyllic evening—my mom was gracious and generous, even to my dad, the air was balmy, the food delicious. My mom had hoped to see the green flash when the sun hit the water, but she wasn't too disappointed when she didn't; she deemed the night perfect, anyway, and it was. I try to go back there in labor, try to see the ocean undulating, the pelicans gliding above us, their great wings open; I try to feel the sand under my feet, smell the salt in the air, see my mom smiling and relaxed, serving up another helping of vinaigrette-kissed orecchiette, but I can't seem to go there beyond snapshots. The whole scene gets swallowed by the wave of the next contraction, the beach and everything on it engulfed in darkness.

A sweet, acrid scent starts to fill the house; a scent I finally identify as burnt sugar. I ask Michael what it could be, and he says it's something the Karens—my midwife and her same-named assistant—are making. I wonder if it's cookies, maybe, or some special tincture that needs sweetening. They have been putting various tinctures and homeopathic remedies under my tongue throughout the labor; I can't tell if these are making any difference, but I appreciate their ministrations. The Karens are wonderful—kind and no-nonsense. It turns out they and Michael have been trying to make the purple rock candy from my story, but the sugar won't stick to the string they've hung inside a jar in our pantry; my "ideal but realistic" story isn't sticking to its own thread. Still, just knowing they wanted to make the treat is a gift. The burnt sugar scent fills me like a balloon, buoys me through the next few contractions.

When my childbirth instructor read my essay a couple of weeks ago, she said, "This is just how it's going to happen, I know it." Somehow even then, I knew she was wrong. I knew I had skewed more toward the "ideal" than the "realistic" portion of the assignment. I knew I had romanticized the birth and everything around it. I have a tendency to do that, to gloss over the darker parts of my experience, to not share the messier parts of myself. To forget how easily things can burn.

Now, though, I am messy. I am pooping in the tub, pooping on the bed. I end up spending most of my labor on the toilet, where I feel more comfortable than anywhere else. I have been vocalizing for sixteen hours at this point, groaning with every contraction. By the time I reach the pushing stage and move onto Karen's wooden birthing stool by the foot of my bed, my throat is raw, but I can't stop, my growls turning even more urgent and animal. When I was in labor with Arin, the nurses told me to stop making sounds after I had been transferred to the hospital; they said it was taking energy away from my pushing. Being quiet seemed painful and impossible, though, as painful and impossible as it was to stop pushing once they decided to wheel me to the operating room. Strange how labor wakes up my voice, even if it's mostly in nonverbal ways.

My sister encourages me over speaker phone as I push; she was unable to get a flight until tomorrow and is at a birth now, herself, but she calls as often as she can, sneaking into the bathroom at the Toronto hospital to talk to me or get updates from Michael. She is a disembodied midwife in the room, saying, "You're doing great, Gayley, you're doing great."

I push for two hours. None of it feels good, the way it had been when I pushed with Hannah. All of it hurts, all of it stings, all of it feels like it is going to kill me. But I keep pushing, sure my tailbone will break or a vital blood vessel in my head will burst. I keep pushing, and eventually I feel a new fullness low in my pelvis, and I remember that this is about a baby, not about me, that this was never about me, that I am going to see my baby soon, and my sister is crying on the phone, and the Karens and Michael are all cheering me on, and I keep pushing and pushing, and some tarry meconium splashes out, which I try not to panic about, and now a head forces its way out of my body, tearing me like cloth, and an eye, one gray eye, slides open, one alert and knowing eye that makes us gasp, and now a body is coming out of my body, a bright pink body whooshing, and here he is on my chest, slick and wet and warm and silent, and my sister is worried by his silence—she hasn't seen his all-seeing eye. She says, "Come on, baby, come on," through the phone; she shouts, "Is he pink? Is he pink?" as Karen rubs him with a blanket, and he cries and cries, and we all cry, too, exhausted and ecstatic, humbled by his wild, fresh beauty.

This is how my "ideal but realistic" story ends: "Michael wraps his arms around both of us as we take our first breaths together as a new family. It is past midnight, no longer Thanksgiving, but it still feels like Thanksgiving to us. We are so thankful for this birthing journey and the journey with Asher that has only just begun."

Aside from the date and time, this is the one part of the story I got right.

[ARLENE stands in front of her triptych, *The Art of Misdiagnosis*. The paintings are large, covered with geometric patterns. On screen, the swirls of paint look muddy, a bit shoddy, but she stands tall, looks proud. These are her masterpieces.]

ARLENE: I was inspired by Sol Lewitt when I was a docent at the Museum of Contemporary Art in Chicago, and in the year 2000, when I painted these pieces, we were having an exhibit of his, and he was one of the first conceptualist artists, the first to say the idea is more important than the art, so it's the idea behind it that I picked up.

He also did something interesting: he wanted to prevent collectors from making money on his art, so he began painting on museum walls so it couldn't be collected; it was there for the exhibit and then it was gone, and it was a very revolutionary idea. I believe it was in the late '50s that he began doing that, and I think the reason I was so drawn to it was the geometric shape. I thought, well, I'm not a trained artist; I don't know how to paint; I can certainly make geometric shapes. So I'm totally self-taught, and what started coming out was, I think, the spirits of my family and the experiences and the medical misdiagnoses in the family.

BUZZ BRANDEIS (FORMER HUSBAND): And at the end of six months, she stopped. She did what she had to do and she was finished. And what she ended up with was a body of work, paintings that are hanging on her wall now that are truly unusual, lovely pieces of art, and I still don't understand how that happened, without the training.

Mom,

Your reference to suicide didn't jar me. Maybe it should have, but it didn't. It didn't seem anywhere in the realm of possibility. The only time you had talked about suicide before was to say that if you ever ran out of money, you would walk into the sea, just walk and walk until the ocean swallowed you up. It didn't seem like a real threat—it seemed like your standard variety of melodrama. And, besides, this time you said that if anything happened, it wouldn't be suicide. I was certain you would never do harm to yourself; you were the most self-protective person I knew. I was more worried about what you'd do to other people, namely Dad.

The police didn't do anything. When we called to say you had returned with Arin, they dropped the case. They talked me out of requesting an involuntary psychiatric hold. "You wouldn't do that to your own mother, would you?" the woman on the phone asked.

It reminded me of when I was assaulted in a movie theater in college—a man, the only other person in the auditorium, had buried his dick in my ponytail, yanking my head back as he pleasured himself with my hair—and the police officer I spoke with on the phone encouraged me to not press charges. He said it would be embarrassing for me to have a masturbation case attached to my name. I listened to him. I let him intimidate me into silence. Now, I stayed silent all over again. How could I think of doing such a thing to my very own mother?

You were sure Dad was orchestrating some way to lock you up forever, to keep you from telling the truth about his dastardly deeds. You didn't trust any of us, and as I tiptoed around you, unsure how to deal with your delusions, my trust in myself started to erode, too.

NOVEMBER 23, 2009

My sister and mom arrive in the morning. I am in bed with the baby when I hear Michael answer the door; the bedroom is dim even though it is sunny outside—there is only one sliver of window high on the wall, which the owner has shaded with cloth napkins clothes-pinned to a dowel. I didn't sleep much—even when Asher slept, I couldn't stop staring at him, couldn't stop thinking that if I did stop looking at him, something horrible would happen. We have two bassinets so we can sleep with Asher safely—one that attaches to the side of the mattress, the other a little foam contraption wedged between our pillows on the bed—but even so, and even after years of sharing a bed with my older kids when they were little, I worry that somehow I will roll on top of him if I let myself nod off.

My mom and sister both have their hands over their hearts as they enter the room. They walk toward me and Asher slowly, reverently, like they are walking down the aisle at a wedding. Both of them have tears in their eyes. In the picture Michael snaps as they reach the bed, I am beaming up at my mom, unguarded, unafraid, and she is beaming back at me. I feel her love and it feels sweet; this moment feels sweet, all of us shifting to gaze at this brand-new person breathing on my chest, his gray eyes gazing right back at us.

"Do you want to hold him?" I ask my mom.

"Of course," she says softly.

My sister scoops him out of my arms and puts him in my mom's.

"Oh!" she gasps, face alight, as she receives him. She coos and bounces and sways her body so he won't cry, and I imagine her looking at me the same way when I was a baby, comforting me with the same movements. I let myself be comforted by this all over again. I think back to my baby shower—more of a mother's blessing—at my friends Nancy and Jenn's house a couple of months earlier. My collected friends had massaged my feet, rubbed fragrant oils into my hands. My mom had brushed my hair, the first time she had done so in years, and it felt so sweet and loving, so motherly when I was no longer used to her being motherly, it melted my heart. My heart melts again now as I watch her cradle my new baby.

Then Asher closes his eyes and something shifts in my mom's face.

"Why did he fall asleep?" she asks, panicky, and shoves the baby back into Elizabeth's arms.

"I have to take a shower," my mom says. "I have to wash my clothes. There is stuff on me a baby should never be near."

After she leaves to clean up, I whisper, "She thinks she poisoned him, didn't she?" to my sister. Elizabeth hands Asher back to me; I pull the neckline of my shirt down beneath my breast and he settles in to nurse. Even though I know my mom is delusional, I lean down and smell Asher's head to check for fumes.

"Oh, Gayley," Elizabeth says. "I know you said it was bad, but I wasn't ready for this."

Elizabeth tells me that when our mom pulled up to the curb at the airport, she had a flannel nightgown wrapped around her nose and mouth to avoid breathing in fumes pumped through the air conditioning vents. A Jack in the Box cup full of urine sat in the cup holder of her car; she wanted to have it tested to see what sort of poison she was being subjected to. She had actually gone to a hospital in North Hollywood during the night because she thought she was having a heart attack; she told Elizabeth she wasn't sure how she got to the ER—it was as if she had driven in a fugue state. Apparently they didn't do a urine test—she was looking for someplace else to take her pee.

I put my hand over my mouth. "What do we do?" I ask. Why hadn't the hospital realized she needed psychiatric help? Why hadn't they kept her there?

"I don't know." My sister sinks onto the bed beside me. "I don't know."

.   .   .   .

We have a restless night. My mom sleeps on the hardwood floor in the living room—she has forgotten her cushion, tells us the floor is good for her back—and the motion sensor lights outside, triggered by cats and raccoons, keep startling her, make her think she's about to be interrogated; she keeps waking up Elizabeth, who is sleeping on the couch, since Hannah is still at Matt's. I, half asleep, think Asher's ear is his mouth, that it's frozen open in some sort of tortured rictus, and wake Michael up with my gasp. Asher keeps waking us up with his sweet kitten cries. All of us are exhausted and edgy in the morning. Michael wanders bleary eyed into the shower. Elizabeth takes Asher from my arms and walks around the house, singing softly to him.

My mom suddenly turns frantic. "What's that?" Her head darts back and forth like a cartoon spy's.

"What is what?" I ask her. *That* could be anything.

"It sounds like an Islamic chant!" She looks ready to bolt.

I listen for a moment. "Oh," I laugh. "That's Michael." He's singing in the shower. "If I Were a Rich Man." I sing a bit of the "*Ya da da da da da dum*" part along with him, which I suppose sounds a bit like a muezzin's call to prayer. Michael and I met doing a musical, but he's not the best singer; he can be a bit nasal, a bit droney.

My mom laughs lightly, too, but she still looks haunted—whether by the Middle Eastern men she thinks are following her, or by "If I Were a Rich Man," itself, by what a rich man she thinks my dad is, by what a rich woman she knows she'd be if only he weren't hiding his fortune from her, I can't say.

"I know this sounds fanciful," she starts, and I wish it did, I wish her stories sounded fanciful. Fanciful stories would involve things like unicorns, not poison, although the unicorns she collected in the '80s weren't really fanciful, either. The schnauzer-sized one that still sits on her coffee table is wooden, muscular, with a lethal brass horn.

[ELIZABETH sits alone on ARLENE's patio. She wears a
large green pendant that rests just below her throat. You
can't see how upset she is to be doing this interview,
how much she doesn't want to be here. She looks cool and
collected, as always; her hair is short and chic. On the
screen, it looks darker than usual.]

ELIZABETH: Well, I've always seen my mother as a very
    creative person and, um, somebody who's always been
    very engaged with art and the arts, and so I think
    seeing this outpouring of creativity from her just
    feels like an extension of who she is, but a real
    manifestation of that creativity. So, um, I think
    when she was starting the process of assembling the
    supplies and finding space, I didn't know what to
    expect or what might come of that process, but I
    think it's become a part of her identity, and while
    she's been an artistic person her whole life, kind
    of assuming this identity as an artist has awakened
    something or satisfied something in her that's been a
    pleasure to watch.

Mom,

I know we planned an intervention, but I don't remember anything about the plans, themselves. I think we had lined someone up, ready to ambush you with help, but none of us remember the details. Maybe Matt remembers, but that door is locked. I just have a vague memory of sitting with Matt in a psychologist's office, one with large windows overlooking the 10 freeway. Why this particular psychologist, I don't know. Someone must have recommended him. I remember a glass coffee table, Hannah's car seat next to it on the floor. I remember the psychologist mostly asked questions; I remember thinking he wasn't very helpful. I wanted answers, tools, not more questions. I remember thinking we had wasted our money, and living on student loans and food stamps, we didn't have much money to waste. I don't know if he was the person we enlisted to do the intervention, don't remember if we had any faith in him at all.

However far along we were in the process, you caught wind of it. You ran away. Nothing scared you more than the thought of ending up in a psychiatric hospital. It was a relief and a worry to have you gone.

Dad flew out to California to help track you down; we found out later you had flown back to Chicago the same day, your planes likely passing mid-air. You tore through Dad's closets and pockets and briefcase; you talked your way into his office downtown and tore through his desk. You looked frantically for evidence and thought you found it—evidence that made sense to no one but you, more "hand notes" you were ready to toss in my face like snow.

In my memory, we tried—somehow—to get you help again, and you ran off again. In my memory, you ended up in a small town in Canada, a small town by a lake. It wasn't clear if it was near Guelph, where Elizabeth had moved with her Canadian boyfriend, Craig, where they had eloped to make it easier for her to stay there, where they were expecting their first baby. If I recall correctly, you likened the place you had landed to the town in Northern Exposure, Dad's favorite TV show. I think you wanted to make him jealous. I don't know what you did there—walked around the lake? ate eggs in a little diner? drank beer with lumberjacks?—I don't know if you even really were there. But you surfaced eventually, and after Elizabeth gave birth on her own 22nd birthday—what would have been Dad's mom Molly's 110th birthday—you went to visit baby Mollie.

You had a knack for bringing postpartum chaos to your daughters. While you were at her house, Elizabeth found a piece of paper that had fallen out of your purse. It was a suicide note. It said that you should have killed our dad before you killed yourself. Elizabeth confronted you, and you laughed it off, calling it a joke. You were just letting off steam, you said. We were all freaked out, but we tried to not take it too seriously. It was too horrible to think about it being real.

NOVEMBER 24, 2009

I spend much of the day curled in bed with the baby, slipping in and out of sleep. The cloth napkins that drape the high window don't let in much light, casting a murky aquarium glow through the room. The still-full birthing pool in the corner sends wavery reflections onto the wall, amplifying the underwater effect; it's starting to smell a bit swampy in here, too. I'm starting to smell a bit swampy, myself.

I try to get up as little as possible—to avoid my mom and walking, both; the stitches make me feel like I have a bowling ball between my legs. Every once in a while, voices drift in from the other side of the closed door, primarily my sister and mom arguing. Elizabeth tries to stay calm, to be the voice of reason, saying things like, "That's just a theory, Mom, not a fact," but their voices often rise, and then they retreat to the cat-pissy laundry room, as far away from the bedroom they can get inside the house to keep from waking me and the baby. Now, though, they are right outside the room, bickering softly. A phone rings, and I hear my sister say, "Thank you for calling me back." Her voice grows fainter as she walks away.

The door flies open and crashes against wall, startling Asher off my breast.

"Why would she do something like that?" my mom asks, wild eyed. "She knew I had a plan!" She thinks Elizabeth called, Sandra, our mom's therapist. Our mom's therapist, who it appears—like seemingly everyone our mom has talked to—believes our mom's story about her deceitful husband.

Adrenalin jitters through me; I hope it won't spike my milk. "Could you please not involve me in this?" I ask. "I need to rest." Somehow this sounds pitiful in my own ears, a weak excuse. My mom storms out of the room.

She runs outside to chase Elizabeth down. Michael follows her to see what is going on. He watches her run up Buena Vista Street, then run even faster back toward the house, terrified. She saw a white truck, she tells him. White trucks are supposedly following her again, almost sixteen years after Hannah's birth. She races back inside.

Elizabeth returns shortly after, and I can hear our mom light into her about calling Sandra.

"It was Dad," Elizabeth tells her. "Dad called me back."

"Liar," our mom hisses.

"Oh, so now I'm one, too?" Elizabeth asks. "If you can't trust the people who love you, who can you trust?"

When I venture out of the bedroom, I learn my mom is trying to figure out her Thanksgiving plans. She has to get away, she says. She can't spend Thanksgiving with my dad, who is planning to come here in two days to meet Asher.

My mom has a long-standing beef about Thanksgiving. When I was married to Matt, we would spend Thanksgiving at his mom's house—she made the most delicious creamed pearl onions, the most delicious yams swimming in butter and brown sugar; she set the most beautiful table, with gold-rimmed goblets she inherited from her mother that look exactly like the ones my mom inherited from hers. My mom was invited every year after she moved to California, but only attended once. Matt and the kids and I usually went to Oceanside for another Thanksgiving meal a day before or after, but my mom always felt like a second-class citizen, a second choice. And she was; my mother-in-law's Thanksgiving had become our bellwether.

One year, she spent Thanksgiving at the Golden Door, an expensive spa in Escondido. Elizabeth and I went to visit her there; all the guests in the dining room were dressed in white robes. Elizabeth said it felt like visiting her at a sanitarium; everyone was hushed, moving slowly, like terry-cloth-clad ghosts, everyone spaced out from a regimen of massage and yoga and very few calories. We were served a cup of vegetable consommé. In my memory that was it, the whole meal, but there must have been more, little plates of artfully arranged vegetables, perhaps a cube of tofu, a spear of pineapple or two.

She thumbs through her large brown leather datebook and lands on her friend Richard in La Jolla. She knows him from one of her cultural associations—the opera, maybe, or the art museum. "Funny little Richard." She shakes her head. "He has such a crush on me."

As she punches his number into her flip phone, her demeanor changes. She stands a little taller, takes a deep breath as if she's about to sing. "Richard!" she cries, her voice loud, terrifyingly chipper. It's as if she's flipped some sort of switch, clicked herself into an Auntie Mame sort of frequency, a jovial socialite, someone who would call the guests "Darling" at dinner parties. "It's me, Arlene. Can you believe it?"

Her whole face has transformed, lit up. She becomes this character fully, this outgoing grande dame, this bon vivant. Elizabeth and I look at each other in disbelief.

"Are you free for Thanksgiving?" she asks. "I'd love to make dinner for you, all the trimmings." She gives a jocular laugh, a sort of feminine Santa's *ho ho ho.* "I *am* known for my stuffing," she says with a sly tone in her voice that makes me cringe even as I am flooded with an intense craving for her butter and vegetable broth-drenched stuffing made with celery and onion and a bag of cubed bread from Pepperidge Farm. One year, home from college, I had my wisdom teeth removed the day before Thanksgiving. Even though my mouth ached, even though I could only chew with my front teeth, I must have eaten a good third of her black Dansk casserole dish full of mushy bready goodness.

She hangs up the phone and her demeanor changes again, turns icy. "At least someone wants me for Thanksgiving." She glares at us. "Too bad it's not my daughters."

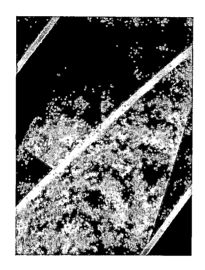

MISDIAGNOSIS I: It Was Not Rheumatic Fever

ARLENE: Well, I was thought to have rheumatic fever
as a child. I missed most of first and second grade
because I always had joint pain; I had this funny
heartbeat that turned out to be a floppy valve from
Ehlers-Danlos. I guess that's what all people have
with mitral-valve prolapse, but they thought it was a
murmur and I was on bed rest, and you know, I didn't
find out until forty years later. You know, this was
the mid-'40s when I was thought to have rheumatic
fever, and it wasn't until the mid-'80s, when my
younger daughter was diagnosed with Ehlers-Danlos
syndrome and this rheumatologist who came in and
felt my skin said, Oh, you have it too. Well, then
the search began. What is this? Well, what am I
dealing with?

RE: SEARCH I

Postmortem Diagnosis

2015

I've always loved research. Pre-Internet, I'd be in the library at least once a week, looking up something that had sparked my interest or would help bring authentic detail to my fiction—'70s feminist performance art, say, or Zen parenting or Santeria or recipes for tagine. Post-Internet, like most of us, I'm always following my curiosity down one rabbit hole after another.

I didn't have that impulse when my mom's delusions started. I didn't research delusion; I didn't scour the Psychology stacks. Looking back, I see myself as strangely incurious about the roots of her behavior. Maybe I was in denial. Maybe her transformation seemed impossible to unpack, too big and wild to even try to begin to understand. Maybe the delusions seemed like something she could control—a willful act—not like something that was controlling her, something that could be looked up in a book. Maybe having a newborn and a toddler simply didn't leave much head space for investigation.

We first hooked up to the Internet in 1995, about two years after Hannah was born, two years after my mom had started acting strange; even then, I didn't search for information that could illuminate her situation. Two years in, we had learned to live with the ups and downs of her "episodes." Some of the time she was fine—a loving nana, a generous mom; when she wasn't, we waited it out as best we could. Nothing we had tried had worked as far as getting her help, not talking to psychologists, not talking to her, so we walked on eggshells, worked on our own patience, tried to set our own boundaries—something I was never good at; something she rarely respected.

Now, I can't seem to stop researching delusion.

I learn the average age of onset of delusional disorder (which seems the most likely diagnosis) is forty (although one study puts it at fifty-five; my mom was fifty-four when hers began).

I learn the most common delusion subsets are:

- erotomanic type, in which the person irrationally believes someone, usually someone famous, is in love with them
- grandiose type, in which the person believes they deserve adulation for some special talent or insight
- jealous-type, in which the person insists their partner is being unfaithful because of delusional "evidence" (this type regularly leads to violence)
- somatic, in which the person has some sort of delusion related to the body: imagining bugs crawling on their skin, for example, or imagining one of their limbs isn't truly their own and should be amputated
- persecutory type, where the person believes they are being victimized in some way. This is the most common form of delusional disorder, and is sometimes combined with grandiose type. Those two together seem to describe my mom to a T. They seem like even more of a fit after I learn that people with delusional disorder often appear to be fine and functional in most aspects of their daily life, and are often involved in formal litigation against imagined persecutors.

In his article, "Delusional Disorder," James A. Bourgeois details some familiar-sounding characteristics of delusional litigants: "determination to succeed against all odds, tendency to identify the barriers as conspiracies, endless drive to right a wrong, quarrelsome behaviors, and saturating the field with multiple complaints and suspiciousness."

I learn it can be hard to treat a delusional disorder, but Pimozide, an antipsychotic drug used since the 1970s, has a 68.5 percent recovery rate. My sister and I used to fantasize we could sprinkle some sort of med in Mom's ubiquitous bottles of diet peach Snapple or cups of decaf. This one sounds like it could have helped.

I also learn from Bourgeois that people with delusional disorder share similar traits with hypochondriacs, in that "both selectively attend to available information. . . . They make conclusions based on insufficient information, attribute negative events to external personal causes, and have difficulty in envisaging others' intentions and motivations."

When I turned thirteen, my friends gave me a thick paperback copy of *A Dictionary of Symptoms*, with the inscription "Happy birthday, you hypochondriac."

As my eyes filled with tears, I heard Laura whisper to Jessica, "She doesn't think it's funny."

She was right; I didn't think it was funny. I thought it was horrible and mean, and as soon as they went home, I couldn't put the book down. I never would have admitted this, but they had given me the perfect gift. Before the end of the day, I was convinced I had colon cancer, rheumatoid arthritis, and peritonitis. I was truly sick at the time and would soon be diagnosed with Crohn's disease, but had definitely acquired some hypochondriac tendencies along the way.

Perhaps my mom and I were more similar than I had realized.

Mom,

Because I didn't know what else to do right after your delusions surfaced, didn't know how else to help you, I turned to my default—writing. I wrote you a letter. The scariest, hardest letter I had ever written in my life. I wrote it in green felt-tipped marker on stationery sized sheets of white paper, folded in half down the vertical center, like a book, so it would fit in a standard envelope. When I found the letter in your drawer all these years later, the seal broken, I could barely look at it; it made my heart race, my hands tremble the way they did when I first sat down to write it.

Dear Mom,

I'm sorry you have been going through such a difficult, painful time lately. It breaks my heart to see you and Dad hurting so much. I am writing to you because I have found it difficult to say what I'm really feeling when I talk with you. Please know that love is behind every word I'm writing.

I know you are convinced that Dad has betrayed you, that he has stolen your security and is hiding from you what is rightfully yours. You have asked me to keep an open mind about this, and I have listened to you, but I am convinced that you are terribly wrong. I do not believe for one minute that he is capable of doing the things you accuse him of. I have looked at your "proof," and it does not say to me what it says to you. I think you have chosen to interpret the papers to fit into your own scenario. You have created a very elaborate plot in your mind about what you think has happened, and are able to twist anything around so it fits into your story line. I think it is highly imaginative and creative, this plot you've concocted—it has all the elements of a good spy thriller, but, like a Tom Clancy novel, I think that it is not based in fact. I believe you have found some compelling clues and some strange

coincidences, but you have read into them things that are just
not there.

I know you are following your instincts, and instincts are
something to heed, I agree, but they are not always right. I have a
stellar example for you. This is going to be hard to tell you, because
I have not told this to anyone before except Matt, and he, only
recently. You went on a similar research binge when I was sick and
you thought you were following your instincts, then. Had you been
truly in touch with your own instincts, and with me, you would
have realized that I was prolonging my illness. Being sick was safe
for me—I didn't have to deal with the regular issues of adolescence
because I was dealing with being sick; as "the sick one," I could be
a hero, I could get pity, compassion, attention, a sort of unhealthy
spotlight. While I probably wouldn't have admitted it then, I
enjoyed playing that role. My x-rays were normal during my
later hospitalization because I wasn't really sick. I know this will
come as a shock to you, but I went out of my way to make myself
ill. I lied about being constipated for all those days—I was really
pooping pretty normally—and, later, I even took laxatives a few
times to give myself diarrhea so I would seem sick. I was scared of
getting better, I was scared of losing the attention I had as "the sick
one." If you had really listened to your instincts, if your instincts
had been true, you would have realized that I was a scared girl—
I was scared of growing up, becoming a woman, scared of taking
on responsibility for my own life. If your instincts were really
valid, you wouldn't have denied so vehemently that there was any
psychological element to my illness. If we had come to terms with
the fact that psychological problems are nothing to be ashamed
of, if I had admitted to myself what I was truly feeling and doing,
I could have gotten well sooner. It has taken me years to come
to terms with that part of my life, and I realize now how I was
running away from the truth. This is probably hard for you to hear,
because as much as that time was difficult for you, too, I know that
you found some meaning and fulfillment in researching various

ailments and bucking the medical system—but your research was based on my own unreality.

I can't help but see parallels to the situation you're in now. I am impressed by the research you've done, and the connections you have made, but I think that they, too, are based in unreality. Please try to examine this possibility. Just as I could have spared us unnecessary concern about my health, I think that you could spare you and Dad unnecessary pain. It is unfair to consider your entire marriage a sham. I don't doubt that you and Dad have some issues to work on together in your marriage, but instead of dealing with the issues themselves, you are hiding behind this plot you have created and are refusing to take any responsibility for the emotional and financial state of your marriage. I really think you owe it to yourself, to Dad, to me and Liz, to examine real issues, putting aside your conspiracy theory. If you could truly see how devastated Dad is by all this, I think you would know that your accusations are untrue. I love you so much and I want you to be happy. If you truly feel the need to divorce, let it be for real reasons, and not for some constructed scenario (and I hope, that if you are able to see past your scenario, you could also see that the marriage is worth saving). I hope this letter has not been too difficult for you to read. It is important to me to say what is in my heart, and I have felt like I have not been very open in our communication lately. I hope we can start fresh now, able to communicate on a real, adult level.

I love you, Mom.

Love,
Gayle

P.S. As I read over this letter, I realized that you may take the part about my illness personally, that you may think I deliberately lied to you at the time, that I caused you unnecessary pain, even humiliation. I want you to know that none of what I did was directed at you. I was very confused—as are most thirteen-year-olds—and I was not seeing things clearly. As I said

before, it has taken me years to work through what happened then,
and it has been the most difficult thing for me to come to terms
with in my life. It has only been in the last couple of years that I've
been able to think of myself as a healthy person. Please don't take
my confession as an attack against you—I am telling you both
so I can come clean with you and to show you that things are not
always as they seem. It is very scary for me to admit these things to
you. Please take the admission in the spirit it is given—with love
and humility. I love you so much. ♡ g
  Matt, Hannah, and Arin send their love too

You never responded to the letter. You didn't say a word to acknowledge you had received it. Years later, when you started talking again
about how valiantly you had fought against the medical establishment when I was sick, I tried to remind you of what I had revealed
in this letter; you shot venom with your eyes and spit out "Well,
that's crazy. If you did that, you were crazy!" You refused to talk
about it ever again. You continued to maintain your side of the
story on camera in your documentary. But I need to talk about it,
Mom—I need to talk about that confusing, painful period of my
life, and this time, you can't stop me.

NOVEMBER 24, 2009

My older kids come to meet their baby brother. Nine months ago, when I told Arin I had news as we sat in a back booth at Mi Tortilla, he guessed I was pregnant and was very sweet about it; when I broke the news to Hannah as we were driving down the freeway, she almost jumped out of the car. As soon as she sees the baby in real life, though, she melts. Both kids gaze at Asher with such wonder and love, my heart nearly bursts. My beautiful babies, all together.

We sit down to dinner, the table covered with aluminum take-out containers full of red sauce–heavy pasta delivered by the local pizza place. My mom, still in the same purple turtleneck and black pants she wore yesterday, looks disheveled and sweaty; disconcerting, as she normally takes great pains with her appearance. After we eat, she corners Arin and tells him she'll give him a hundred dollars to drive her to her friend's house in Carlsbad, an hour and a half away. She doesn't tell him she's scared to take her own car because she thinks it's being followed by numerous Middle Eastern men. She doesn't tell him she's been driving as if she's in *The Bourne Identity*—her own words—to escape them. He agrees—he has to study for an exam at UC Riverside, but who wouldn't want a quick hundred dollars? When my mom goes to the bathroom, Elizabeth and Michael swoop in to caution him about her current state. His face drops.

"I'm sorry, Nana," he says when she returns. "If we leave now, I won't be back until 11, and I have a lot of homework."

My mom immediately charges toward my sister. "Sabotage!" she yells, one arm in the air as if she's rattling a saber. Michael steps in between them.

"We're going to a hotel," he says firmly. "You can't come into my house and talk to people like that." Michael's face and voice both sharpen; I've never seen him like this before, my normally placid, mild husband. The papa bear in him rising up, protecting his clan. It's both terrifying and exhilarating.

My mom grabs Elizabeth's batik scarf, the one she bought during a trip to Sausalito with an ex-boyfriend many years ago, and throws it over her head.

"You don't know how dangerous this is for me," she says, her entire face covered, then races out the door into a world where she thinks she's being chased and drugged and conspired against.

For a moment, we're all silent. It's as if she's pulled all the oxygen out of the house behind her.

"Fuuuck," I say under my breath, not a word that often comes through me. We all stare at each other, eyebrows raised, reeling. Then Arin points to my arms and says, "Look! A baby!" and everyone laughs and the oxygen whooshes back in.

The rest of the night feels like a party. The kids start messing with instruments. Arin puts on Hannah's blue Snuggie and looks like some sort of crazed monk as he plays guitar, swaying wildly in his chair. My sister and I sit side by side on the piano bench, laughing so hard, I'm worried the stitches in my perineum will pop. Then Arin starts to play the Belle and Sebastian song "Get Me Away from Here, I'm Dying," and Elizabeth and I turn to each other and burst into tears.

"What if that's the last image we ever have of her?" I ask and we fall into each other, the baby nestled between us.

MISDIAGNOSIS II: It Was Not Crohn's Disease

ARLENE: The second panel is about my older daughter, who
   was treated for Crohn's disease all through her teen
   years. From the time she was thirteen, she was thought
   to have Crohn's disease, so I call this *Misdiagnosis
   II: Not Crohn's Disease, Acute Intermittent Porphyria*.
   Well, it wasn't until six years of being mistreated
   for Crohn's disease by some of the world's best
   doctors, um, a young woman from India, a doctor she
   saw when she was in her first year of college, said,
   "Well, have you ever been tested for porphyria?" We
   hadn't even known the name, and she took this twenty-
   four-hour urine test.

[The camera lingers lovingly on a close-up of
ARLENE's painting; it looks kind of like she used the
sponge-painting technique that was all the rage on the
walls of massage studios for a while.]

Mom,

I always had a touchy stomach, but when I was thirteen and we moved from our beloved apartment across the street from Lake Michigan in Evanston to a yellow aluminum-sided ranch-style house in Winnetka, my belly took a turn for the worse; I was doubled over or in the bathroom much of the time. You would ask me not to flush—you would come in, peer at the toilet bowl as if you were reading tea leaves. I wouldn't be surprised if you kept detailed charts.

Dr. Stein, who looked like Mr. Hooper from *Sesame Street*, thought I was lactose intolerant. We switched to sweet acidophilus milk at home, which seemed to help for a while and was much easier to swallow than the goat's milk you bought at first. Then the pain and trips to the bathroom ratcheted up again, and you trotted me back to the doctor. This time, he thought I might have irritable bowel syndrome, perhaps triggered by the stress of our recent move.

"Oh, no," you insisted. "No, Gayle is very well adjusted."

I fought back tears. I hadn't wanted to move, even though you had bought the house after I told you I heard it was unsafe to go to the bathroom at Evanston Township High School, which I was slated to attend the following year. Supposedly girls would steal lunch money from other girls at knifepoint, but I imagined this was apocryphal, or at least rare, certainly not reason enough to leave the apartment I loved, the only home I had known. And despite your assertions, I hadn't adjusted well to our tony new suburb. I had taken to lying—lying about Dad's age, saying he was in his forties instead of his sixties; lying about being Jewish, telling kids we just hadn't decided which church to join in the area yet; lying about which level I had reached in figure skating competition, saying I could do a double axel when the best I could do was a double flip, and then only sometimes, and sloppily. Not that this made any difference to my fellow eighth graders; I was still the weird, quiet new girl with protruding eyeteeth who always had to go to the bathroom in the middle of class.

You were determined to get a different diagnosis. You learned that the "foremost authority on GI issues" (a phrase you often repeated) was at the University of Chicago, the campus where you and Dad first met. Soon we were spending time, lots of time, at Billings Hospital, a giant Gothic building that could easily serve as a haunted castle on film, at least from the outside. The inside was all gleam and squeak, all X-ray hum and alcohol fume. Site of my degradation; site of my transformation. The place where barium would be shot up my ass, and scopes shoved down my throat; the place where I would be changed, superhero-like, into a mythical creature known as the Sick Girl, you as my trusty sidekick. It was your calling—Mother of the Sick Girl. You had never been more ready for an assignment. In truth, if anyone was a sidekick, it was probably me.

When I was diagnosed with Crohn's disease, a chronic inflammatory bowel disease, you seemed thrilled. A diagnosis with the word "disease" in its name; something serious, with no known cure; something that couldn't be chalked up to nerves. And I have to admit, I was a bit thrilled, too.

My doctor seemed to know that. During a proctoscopy, I felt something spurt between my legs as I stood against an upright screen, the scope working its way up my rectum. It sounded like when you squeeze the last bit of shampoo out of a plastic bottle. When I pulled up my panties—which had been yanked down to my knees—there was a cold goopy mass on the cotton. It felt rotten against my skin.

"You had a little *moment* there, didn't you?" the gastroenterologist smirked, one eyebrow raised.

I hadn't felt any pleasure, but he was on to something. I never would have admitted this, but being sick had become a turn-on for me. Not a physical turn-on. More of an emotional turn-on. Maybe even a spiritual turn-on. Perhaps that goop *was* orgasmic in an ectoplasmic kind of way. My sad little spirit getting its rocks off. You right there with me, feeling your own crescendo of purpose.

After the diagnosis, I no longer had to ask my teachers for permission to run to the bathroom. After the diagnosis, I became a celebrity of sorts, especially once I started high school that fall at New Trier West. Teachers and popular girls visited me during my hospitalizations; my classes sent me cards and flowers, even a male belly dancer (who I was too embarrassed by to properly enjoy). I knew "The Sick Girl" was as close to the "It Girl" as I was going to get, and I relished it. I milked it. I turned myself into a veritable Sick Girl industry. I became the youngest board member of the local chapter of the National Foundation for Ileitis and Colitis, and wrote a column for their newsletter, geared toward young sufferers of the disease. When this platform felt too small, I created my own handwritten *Gastro-Intestinal Gazette*, which you photocopied for me, and mailed off to my handful of subscribers (obtained after you convinced the NFIC to write an article about me). I even invented a board game—The Road to a Healthy Digestive System, using a piece of cardboard as the base, then pasting a brightly color-penciled drawing of a digestive tract onto the center. I was quite proud of that drawing, which I had done while eyeing an anatomy book. The large intestine and rectum were an electric blue, the small intestine pink as a pig. The esophagus and stomach were deepening shades of purple, the liver and pancreas dark and light green.

The game was laid out like a Monopoly board, squares all along the edges that said things like, "Take your Prednisone—move ahead two spaces," or, "Sigmoidoscopy—go back one space." You could land on a space where you had to pick up an "Upper GI" card, which offered trivia questions about the upper digestive tract, or you could land on a space where you had to pick up a "Lower GI" card with true/false questions about lower bowel function. You were convinced the NFIC would immediately want to mass produce it and I'd become a famous game magnate.

I carefully packaged the game and the cards in a shirt box and brought it with me to my next appointment at the gastroenterologist's office. You and I both knew it was going to wow the doctor, knock his socks off.

When I showed it to him, though, he sighed.

"You're spending way too much time thinking about this disease, Gayle," he said. "You need to focus on your real life."

I was shocked and insulted that he would say such a thing. The disease *was* my real life. It had become my identity, my calling card, my *raison d'etre*. I packed the game back up and held it close to my chest.

You shared my indignation. You sent letters about my game to all the major toy companies, all the G-I related foundations, all the big research hospitals. You talked to a relative who used to design Cracker Jack toys and had produced one board game with Milton Bradley—"Feeley Meeley" (subtitle: *"the game that gives you a FUNNY FEELING!"*) where a player draws a card, then reaches blindly into a box and finds the object on the card through touch alone.

"This is a guaranteed money maker," you wrote in your pitch letter. "Over a million people have Inflammatory Bowel Disease in this country, and they want a game that they can relate to."

No one jumped on the idea, which confounded us both.

"Don't let them stop you," you assured me. "Nothing's going to get in our way."

I wanted to believe you. But something did get in our way, or at least threaten to. I started to get well. After a year of medication that gave me a moon face and hairy arms and the constant taste of metal in my mouth, I started to get well. Less pain. Fewer trips to the bathroom.

This would not do. This would not do at all.

NOVEMBER 25, 2009

The Karens left us with a bag of little unguents and creams, herbal salves for cracked nipples and sore perineums, a tiny round jar of golden powder to help dry up Asher's umbilical stump. When Arin and Hannah were babies, the belly button process seemed to take weeks—smelly, oozy weeks of swabbing around the stump with alcohol, being careful to not irritate it with the edge of their diapers. With just a couple of days of the sweet smelling pixie dust, Asher's stump has fallen off, leaving a perfect, clean belly button in its wake. It's like magic. Asher is like a magic, cartoon baby—he rubs his eyes with his fists when he's tired; he coos—he actually coos. His skin is so soft, it almost burns my hand. He's like this enchanted little beam of light, as if he doesn't want us to worry about him so we can focus all our worrying on my mom.

Still, I can't help but worry about him, at least a little. I worry I might not be making enough milk, that Asher's nursing latch might be a bit askew. I tell my sister and she asks me if she can take a look. I lift my shirt, and there is a frisson of awkwardness. We haven't seen each other naked since we were little girls, when our bodies were an extension of one another's, when we took baths together, sat on the toilet back to back together, "touched tongues" to feel the electric shock that knocked us both backwards. She reaches out to touch my breast, and it feels like the weirdest thing in the world and the most natural thing in the world all at once.

The bedroom has become even more of a swamp—we still haven't emptied the birthing tub and it's growing more fetid each day. I don't have the energy to figure out how to drain the thing, much less do it; I find myself getting used to its humid boggy breath.

Elizabeth screws up her face, though. "We need to take care of this," she says, and soon a hose is snaking out the high window.

Soon that soup of shit and blood and amniotic fluid is whooshing out of the tub and onto a strip of dead grass.

I watch my sister work, all decisive action and economy of movement. Her long, graceful fingers, her capable midwife hands, always seem to know exactly what to do.

ARLENE: Well, since then, she's had negatives, she's
   had positives. We don't know if that's a definitive
   diagnosis, but that certainly is not Crohn's disease.

Mom,

Sometimes I could feel my edges getting blurry. I wasn't sure where I ended and where the air began. I spent so much time reading and writing—as a sick girl, as a healthy girl—I often lost track of where I really was. I dissolved into ink, became blank as paper. When I wasn't reading, wasn't writing, I wasn't sure who I was. When I was reading, was writing, I wasn't sure who I was, either; I lost myself in the flow of words. I lost myself, in general.

When I looked in the mirror, I often didn't recognize myself. Sometimes I felt like part of me had drifted away into some collective consciousness and I couldn't quite believe I lived inside my particular skin. I would stare at my face, touch my own cheek, and barely grasp that those brown eyes, those funny teeth, belonged to me. I felt like an alien inside my own body.

Pain used to bring me back. It focused my body into sharp relief. It gave me a touchstone, a place to inhabit. But the pain had gone, and I felt lost.

I launched a new tactic: constipation. If I claimed to be constipated, I wouldn't have to show you the contents of the toilet. The longer I went without a "BM," the longer I could hold on to my Sick Girl identity, and the more of a quest I could generate for you. You seemed a little lost without the constant demands of my illness.

One day, two days, didn't seem so bad in your eyes. It was almost a reprieve after all my bathroom racing. But when I got to day four, you began to get gratifyingly concerned. You gave me laxatives, which I pocketed; enemas, which I emptied into the sink.

I started to spritz Love's Baby Soft every time I pooped to mask the smell. Once you swooped in after I flushed but before I had a chance to spray the room.

"It smells a little like BM in here," you said, voice tinged with hope.

"I just windered," I said quickly, our family's term for passing gas.

"At least things are moving in there," you said. When you left the room, I sprayed Love's Baby Soft everywhere, heart pounding. That was close. Too close.

Five days, six. I acted like I was in agony, doubling over like the good old days; you moaned whenever I did, just a hair behind me, a ghostly duet. When you talked to my gastroenterologist, he said the longest one of his patients had gone without a bowel movement was ten days. When the woman finally pooped, my doctor gave her a rose. My doctor, who palpated my belly on day six and said he couldn't feel much stool in my colon. He eyed me suspiciously, and I turned away, cheeks burning, as you said, "Do you think her colon could be paralyzed?"

By day eight, I couldn't keep up the ruse; I finally invited you into the bathroom to see what my body had produced, and you acted as if I had just won an Olympic medal. Still, I wanted my doctor to give me a rose; I wanted him to give me a whole bouquet of roses. Maybe even a tiara. I wanted to be queen of the sick girls forever.

My body, however, was starting to conspire against me. I was starting to gain back the weight I had lost from malabsorption. I was starting to get taller. My legs grew so fast, bright red stretch marks spread from my hips down my thighs, striping me like bacon. And then my period began. This felt like the biggest insult of all.

I hid my period from you. You didn't hide yours from me, occasionally telling me you were hemorrhaging and showing me a toilet bowl full of bright red blood. But I wasn't ready for you to see that I was growing up, to see that I was a normal girl. I wasn't ready to see it myself.

I rigged pads out of folded stacks of yellow Kleenex, then flushed them down the toilet to avoid any trash-can discoveries.

Eventually the pipes clogged, and I feigned confusion when the plumber came and fished out a gruesome yellow wad. I started to buy brick-like pads from the high school bathroom dispenser for a quarter a piece, the kind that came with two little safety pins to secure them to one's underpants. I hid the pads at the bottom of my backpack; after I used them, I wrapped them like mummies in toilet paper and shoved them into a laundry hamper that held my old toys until I had a chance to sneak them out to the big garbage can outside.

One night, you and Dad hosted a business party at our house. I didn't feel like talking to anyone, so I pretended the pain was flaring again. I had just taken a shower to get myself ready, but I put my nightgown back on and crawled back into bed. I could hear chattering and laughing downstairs, could smell wine and whiskey and perfume, and was thrilled to not have to be part of it.

A couple of guests insisted on seeing me, the poor brave sick girl, and you ushered them into my dimly lit room. One woman crouched beside my platform bed and touched my hair. It was still damp, and her hand recoiled. I was thrilled that she probably thought I was clammy with fever, not freshly shampooed.

One of the guests gave me a book: *Books from Writer to Reader*, signed by the author. I was known as a writer throughout my dad's company—his secretary, Doris, often typed up my handwritten stories and poems; coworkers often read them before my dad brought them back home. I had my own little fan base there. I wondered if anyone could tell I was being author of my own illness, author of my own life. It was the best thing I had ever written.

I decided to try another round of "constipation." This time, you convinced my doctor to have me hospitalized. I was excited at first as you checked me in to Billings—back to the place of my Sick Girl reign!—but then I went into the bathroom and realized my latest period wasn't over. Two spots of blood splotched my panties.

A nurse noticed as I climbed into my hospital bed, my gown riding up.

"Want me to get you a pad, honey?" she asked.

"Oh, no," I said, heart racing. No one knew I had my period, and that wasn't going to change now. "It's just a juicy winder."

She had no idea what I was talking about. Apparently not everyone shared my family's vernacular for sharts.

"You sure I can't get you a pad?" she asked, eyebrows raised.

I hoped she hadn't noticed the toilet paper I had tucked inside my underpants. "No, thank you," I said and pulled the sheet up over my body.

All the tests they took during that hospitalization came back normal. I was either in remission, or the Crohn's disease was a misdiagnosis from the start. You insisted it was the latter, especially when my doctor told you, "We think there's a psychological element to Gayle's illness. We think she's lying about the constipation."

"They're crazy," you said to me as you sat at the foot of my bed. "They're crazy if they think you're crazy." I nodded in agreement, tears prickling my eyes.

NOVEMBER 26, 2009

On Thanksgiving day, my mom's green Sonata is not filled with casserole dishes as they were in my "ideal but realistic" birth story, at least not for her family; we have no idea where she might be. She could be with her friend Richard; she could be in Santa Barbara; she could be anywhere. We find ourselves half dreading, half hoping to see her car pull up outside the window. We don't really want her here, but we want to know she's safe.

Elizabeth and I are trying not to worry about our dad, too; he hasn't driven this far on his own in ages. Our mom always drives when they come to visit from Oceanside, over an hour away, but he decided to make the trek in his gold Infiniti. He loves to drive, even though he usually only goes short distances; he is proud of the fact that he just renewed his driver's license for five more years. My dad is no normal ninety-year-old. Most people who meet him think he's seventy; when he was truly seventy, he looked decades younger—he started a whole new advertising career at that age, and worked full time for fifteen more years at an agency that revered him so much, they painted a Warhol-esque mural of him in a conference room. For his ninetieth birthday last month, we surprised him by self-publishing *The Book of Wonders*, a collection of funny and provocative things he wondered about (the first one being "Do birds ever get constipated?"). Before her latest breakdown, my mom helped squire away all his notebooks containing these wonders, and I transcribed and formatted them into a book, a book he wasn't expecting, a book he's now very proud of. He's spry and hilarious and handsome, like a pale Harry Belafonte. When he arrives and sits down, a bit tired from the trip, I lower Asher into his lap. It's an instant love connection. They stare deeply at one another—ninety-year-old to ninety-hour-old. They can't stop staring.

"I'm never going to forget this," my dad says, one eye a little blue from glaucoma, as he and Asher keep their gaze locked. "This is burned into my heart."

In all the chaos, we haven't planned our Thanksgiving meal, although Elizabeth and I had independently pored over Mark Bittman's list of 101 Thanksgiving side dishes on the *New York Times* website last week, and we both thought the pumpkin noodle kugel sounded amazing.

Noodle kugel is one of our mom's signature dishes, but she's never made it for Thanksgiving. Her kugel is luscious, rich with cream cheese and egg, topped with crushed corn flakes, dusted with cinnamon sugar. A couple of years ago, she sent in an audition tape for *The Next Food Network Star*. She billed herself as the "Good for You Chef" and made a kugel with low-fat cream cheese, egg substitute, just a touch of agave nectar for sweetness. In the audition tape, she takes a bite and says *Mmmm,* closing her eyes in a self-conscious swoon, but when she fed it to us, it tasted like cement, heavy and flavorless. Not the dish's usual golden succulence. Still, she was shocked when she wasn't chosen for the show; she later accused Rachael Ray of stealing her "healthy cooking" angle.

Hannah and Arin are at Matt's mom's house, per Thanksgiving tradition, and I miss them terribly. I feel a pang as I think about my former mother-in-law's pearl onions, the gold-rimmed goblets clinking. For twenty years, Patricia was more of a real mom to me than my own mom had been. Part of the reason it took me a long time to leave my first husband was because I didn't want to leave her, too.

Elizabeth makes a run to Gerard's, and returns with an abundance of grocery bags. She bought a turkey breast for herself and our dad—the only meat eaters in the house; it was barbecued in a large drum right outside the market, and smells amazing—smoky and savory. She lugs the bags into the kitchen and gets to work. Michael tries to help, but she shoos him away. "I need this," she says, closing herself behind the kitchen door, giving herself over to the therapeutic properties of knife and cutting board, pan and heat.

She whips up a feast, a true feast, in less than two hours—roasted brussels sprouts, sweet potatoes brightened with orange juice and zest, mashed potatoes with mushroom gravy, stuffing studded with dried cranberries and pecans (some tucked into mushroom caps), fresh green beans with almonds, even the pumpkin kugel we had drooled over in the *New York Times*. There's barely enough room on our small dining table to hold it all.

We eat mostly in silence—other than the near constant stream of "Wow" and "Mmmm" as we try each new dish, followed by a stream of praise for Elizabeth's seemingly miraculous feat.

"This feels like an island in the storm," I say, Asher tucked against my body. I know this phrase is a cliché, and I have no idea what kind of storm might be barreling down upon us, but I am grateful for this island, this lull, this peace. I am grateful to be in a room suffused with love and calm and delicious food, the air warm with all of it.

After we're sure we can't swallow another morsel, Elizabeth brings out a pumpkin pie made at Gerard's. Somehow we manage to devour it, groaning with each sweet, smooth bite.

My dad says he needs to close his eyes before he attempts the drive back to Oceanside. Asher is drifting off in my arms; I know this is my cue to nap, too.

"Why don't we lie down together?" I ask my dad. Elizabeth and Michael wave us off to the bedroom as they start to clear the table.

With the birthing tub gone, the room feels lighter now, fresher. The sun melts, buttery, through the small windows.

My dad slips off his New Balance sneakers, the only shoes he's found that fit his long, flat feet, and climbs into our bed. We changed the sheets right after Asher was born but haven't removed the waterproof mattress cover that was part of our birth preparation supply list; it crackles as my dad slides over to give me room on the pale-purple flannel sheet. I scootch to the center of the bed. My dad falls asleep almost immediately; he sleeps on his back with his mouth open and it freaks me out a bit—he looks so much like a corpse, I check to make sure he's still breathing. Asher, nestled against my side, is asleep, too; so soundly, I keep putting my hand on his chest to check for his breath, as well. As tired as I am, I can't seem to nap. I lie between my dad and my baby—ninety years old, ninety hours old—and it occurs to me this is the purest experience I'll ever have of middle age. Here I am, firmly—sweetly—in the middle of our spacious generations, dead center between the edges of human existence, listening for signs of life.

[CUT to outside shot of Medical Center West Los Angeles,
then back to conference room with DR. NEVILLE PIMSTONE,
gastroenterologist; DESIREE LYON HOWE, founder/executive
director of the American Porphyria Foundation; and MIRA
GEFFNER, porphyria sufferer.]

ARLENE: Now, one other symptom you didn't mention, and I
   know it can be very prevalent, is violent episodes of
   vomiting and regurgitation, and my daughter has had
   episodes like that, where she would become totally
   dehydrated if she didn't get to an emergency room
   setting or have medications that would stop these
   episodes.

[DR. PIMSTONE, HOWE, and GEFFNER all nod in
understanding, and it is strange for said daughter to
watch this, as if she is watching a panel of judges
determining her fate.]

[Cut to screen that says acute porphyria can be
misdiagnosed as Crohn's disease or other inflammatory
bowel diseases.]

ARLENE: Is that very common in porphyria or not as common
   as these other symptoms?

DR. NEVILLE PIMSTONE: I think you've just underscored one
   of the key reasons for guidelines. The symptoms that
   you mention are nonspecific; there are so many reasons
   for vomiting and nausea and abdominal pain that to
   think of porphyria is just one of the many things
   one could think of. There are many more common causes
   for nausea and vomiting, but if one thinks porphyria,
   yes, this can be a presentation because the metabolic

reason for the attack is that the small molecule which goes up in making the porphyrin heme can affect the nervous system which controls the movement, the motility or the movement, of the bowel. It affects the way the stomach empties; it affects the way the small bowel contracts, and that is probably the basis for the abdominal pain that occurs and for the nausea and vomiting that occurs. [Daughter hears this and starts to wonder: Maybe it really is porphyria. . . . Those symptoms do sound familiar. . . .]

Mom,

My constipation tactics may have been a bust, but they left me with an abundant stash of laxatives. I discovered that if I took four of the small pills at a time, I would get diarrhea.

"See," you said to my doctor after I showed you the results in the toilet. "She's not making this up."

"Maybe it's irritable bowel," he said. "Alternating constipation and diarrhea points to it. Maybe that's what it's been all along."

"It's not irritable bowel," you insisted. "She had the cobbleston-ing." You were pretty sure the Crohn's was misdiagnosed, but in my early X-rays the classic Crohn's ulcers had lined my small in-testine like a European road. You didn't want the word "irritable" attached to me—and to you, by proxy.

"She doesn't anymore," my doctor said. "I think you should get her some counseling."

But no, you would have none of that. You were offended he would even suggest such a thing. Instead, you started to look into alternative therapies.

We tried dry brushing and juice fasts, aloe vera juice and acu-puncture. You took me to the Homeopathic Institute, where we ate basmati rice and yellow lentils, and a bearded homeopathic practi-tioner interviewed me so he could know me as a "whole person." This creeped me out. I only wanted him to know my symptoms.

"How is your relationship with your mother?" he asked, as you sat in the chair across from the exam table.

"It's great!" I said brightly, then burst into tears.

"Can you tell me what that's all about?" he asked, visibly amused, but I couldn't.

Not with you right there in the room. Even if you weren't in the room, I wouldn't have known what to say.

· · · ·

You were sure a television movie would be made of our life. Of course you would be the heroic crusader, stopping the evil doctors in their tracks. You would be played by Shirley Jones; people often told you that you looked like a brunette Shirley Jones.

I would be the heroic sick girl, played by Ally Sheedy or Kristy McNichol. I just hoped the camera wouldn't be able to see inside the girl, the careful machinations behind her brave smile.

I wasn't sure how to keep up my Sick Girl charade, but I wasn't ready to let it go, either. Then one day, you asked if I was limping, and I realized I had a new avenue to explore and exploit. I acted as if my leg had turned in at the hip, as if walking was becoming more and more difficult. My doctor thought it could be bone damage from my long-term steroid use, and suggested I use a wheelchair to keep my weight off my hip joint until we figured out what was going on. A wheelchair! Now there was a solid Sick Girl accessory! No need to worry about toilet bowl contents when you have to use a wheelchair! You rented a bright-yellow Amigo mobility scooter for me, and I was able to use the elevator at school, off-limits to students without special permission; I found myself hit with a new wave of attention from kids who had grown immune to my Sick Girl mystique. The Amigo was truly my friend. And it gave me a means of escape. Before the scooter, I didn't really have the energy to go off anywhere by myself, but now I often took the scooter, little engine grinding, into the forest preserve near our house. I would park it by the lagoon, get out and walk amongst the groves of oak trees, leaves sticking to my shoes, their scent sweet against the damp earth. Sometimes a deer would appear on the other side of the water, and I'd stay as still as possible in the dappled light that came through the branches, hoping it would look right into my eyes, that it would bless me, somehow, forgive me. As soon as it noticed me, though, it would run away, and I was sure it could see down to my most rotten core.

· · · ·

You learned of a craniosacral therapist in Milwaukee, and we crossed the state line to visit his office. I didn't have any expectations for this appointment—none of the other alternative therapies had touched me in any real way. This time, though, was different. The office was homey, full of beautiful, inspiring art. It smelled like herbal tea. The young bearded doctor had me lie on my stomach on a massage table, and when he touched a certain part of my back, I started to cry.

"I'm sorry," I said, embarrassed.

"It's okay," he said. "Happens all the time. Emotion is locked in the body. I'm just helping to release it."

That gave me permission to bawl, and it did feel like a release. It felt wonderful. He had me turn over onto my back. He reached behind my neck and started to press into the base of my skull, and my leg, my "funny leg" as we had taken to call it, started to twitch, started to right itself without any conscious effort on my part.

"It's working," you said in awe. "It's a miracle."

I closed my eyes and let myself feel my body coming back into alignment. What in the world had I been doing to myself? Why had I let it go on so long?

After the session was over, I felt lightheaded. I felt light. You drove us to the Public Natatorium for lunch, an old public swimming building that had been transformed into a restaurant with a dolphin tank at its center. We ate our medium-rare burgers in the narrow dining room dripping with ferns, a parrot in a cage behind us, and watched the dolphins jump through hoops and shimmy upright across the pool on their tails. Water flumed up and crashed against the Plexiglas window next to our table. After the show was over, kids were allowed to come and touch the dolphins. I limped to the pool while you stayed with our food. I ran my palm down the slick back of one of the dolphins; I felt its wholeness, the way it lived so fully and joyfully inside its skin, and my heart ached with longing. I knew I was ready. I was finally ready to be well.

NOVEMBER 27, 2009

We start to wonder, to worry, more about my mom. Whenever we try to call her cell, it goes straight to voice mail. Michael remembers she told him she left her phone at the Best Western in Loma Linda the day before Asher was born. She had thought people in the rooms on either side of her were spying on her, had thought a white van in the parking lot was tracking her movements. She had taken the battery out of her phone, had thrown both pieces into a trash bin in her room.

After Michael retrieves the phone from the hotel, we scroll through my mom's contacts to find Richard's number. Michael excuses himself and gives Richard a call in the office while I rest in the bedroom with Asher and Elizabeth. I try to listen to Michael's end of the conversation, but can only hear murmurs through the door.

Michael comes back into the room about fifteen minutes later, teary.

"What's wrong?" I ask, heart accelerating. Elizabeth sits on the bed next to me, looking similarly on edge.

"Why did she choose him?" His voice breaks as he shakes his head in disbelief.

"What happened?" Elizabeth loops her hand into mine, bracing us both.

Michael tells us our Mom had indeed driven down to Richard's the night she stormed away. They had watched a movie, had a bite to eat, went to bed—him upstairs, her downstairs, Richard had assured Michael. The next day, they went to a Greek restaurant. She was worried when a woman had pointed to their table; she was sure the woman would poison her food, and refused to eat it when it arrived. Richard suggested they bring the meals back to his house, suggested they both eat half of each dish so he could prove to her they weren't poisoned. She balked; she insisted the woman wanted to cause her harm.

"Don't do this," Richard had pleaded. He told Michael his first wife had thought coworkers were poisoning her food. She'd lock it up at work so they wouldn't be able to access it. Such a strange coincidence that my mom would show up at his door, thinking her food was poisoned, too. Michael pauses in his telling of the story and takes a deep breath.

"What happened with his wife?" I ask.

"She killed herself," says Michael and a chill travels through my body. Michael looks at me with such concern, I turn my head to avoid breaking down.

"Your mom told him she wanted to have Thanksgiving with her family, after all," Michael says. "Richard was glad; he told her that's where she should be."

"Do you think she drove by and saw Dad's car and took off again?" I ask.

"I wonder." Elizabeth squeezes my hand hard.

Richard is devastated when he learns we have no idea where our mom has gone.

"Poor guy," I say. "He must have been so triggered by all of this." As if I'm not being triggered, myself. As if all of us aren't in shock. Easier to transfer sympathy to a stranger for a moment; easier to worry about someone we don't know.

"Why did she choose him?" Michael asks again. "Of all people in the world, why did she have to choose him?"

The next morning, I get a call from an unfamiliar number with an 818 area code.

"Is this Gayle Brandeis?" a woman asks.

"Yes," I answer and hold my breath.

"Do you know where your mother is?"

My heart starts to race. "No," I say. "Do you?"

The woman tells me she is calling from Sherman Oaks Hospital. She was my mom's nurse, she says; her name is Mary. My mom had come in complaining of chest pain the previous night; she was hooked up to IVs and heart monitors, but had left the hospital abruptly this morning, had torn out the IVs, ripped away the wires. The hospital had notified the police. I was listed as my mom's emergency contact; Mary hoped I would know where she had gone.

"I'm sorry," I tell her. "We're looking for her, too."

I fill her in on what's been happening with my mom for the last couple of weeks, what's been happening for the last sixteen years.

"She's never been diagnosed?" Mary asks.

"She doesn't believe anything's wrong with her," I tell her.

"That's hard," she says. "I'm sorry."

She asks for information about my mom's car; she tells me she'll have the security guards check the parking garage to see if it is still there; if it is, they'll block it in. She gives me the phone number for the police department. She congratulates me on the baby. She wishes me luck.

The Van Nuys police officer on the phone is kind but cursory. He gets all the details about my mom—height, weight, what she might have been wearing. He gives me a case number and his direct line. He says we can call any time. He assures me he'll do his best to find her.

I stare at the string of digits on the yellow Post-It. They make her disappearance feel more real, somehow. This is no longer just a family matter—it's something much bigger; it also feels much smaller somehow now, too, as if she's been reduced to the case number swimming before my eyes. I hope this number will help her get the help she needs, but something in me resists its order, its depersonalization. My mom has always seemed so expansive, too slippery to be contained by anything, but here she is spun down to a tidy little code, something easy for police to file away.

MISDIAGNOSIS III: Not an Eating Disorder, Ehlers-Danlos

[Cut to ARLENE in front of third panel of triptych.]

ARLENE: The panel 3 is about my younger daughter, who,
at the age of twelve, had this horrific experience
with regurgitation. She couldn't keep food down for
seven months and she was diagnosed with Ehlers-Danlos
syndrome. Then the rheumatologist came in and said
it's Ehlers-Danlos syndrome and, you know, "What is
that?" Well, it causes flexible joints; it can cause
joint pain; it's an unusual rare genetic disease.
Well, I had never heard of it and no one in my family
had ever heard of it, and then I was back in the
library trying to do some medical research, but the
doctors in the meantime, in another wonderful well-
respected teaching hospital, said, "She has an eating
disorder. We have to put her in the psychiatric ward."
(ARLENE clasps her hands in front of her, makes a

funny smirk.) I said, "This is crazy, this is the most mainstream kid you could ever hope to find. She has loads of friends; she's not a people pleaser; she's very much her own person." I said, "This is not an eating disorder." Well, I become immediately like the scourge of the doctors. (Laughs) I said they were wrong, and, uh, I guess you're not supposed to do that, but I did. And so the battle began with the doctors; I was the "controlling mother" [ARLENE gives a look like "How could they ever say this?"], trying to control the medical team. In the meantime, I said—and I had no support for what I believed, I mean, I didn't have support from anyone—she continued to lose weight. She was really in terrible shape, and I was just going off the wall.

Mom,

I still miss our old Evanston apartment, the apartment you so resented—5B, on the fifth floor of the five-story red brick building, 550 Sheridan Square. It's what I still think of when I think of "home" at its most archetypal level. You didn't think we should be renting—you wanted to buy a house. You never let Dad forget this, even though he tried to explain to you that his company was going through bankruptcy and having assets would be risky. I am glad we didn't buy a house then; I loved Sheridan Square. It wasn't actually a square, just half of one, that L-shaped, one-way street that started in Evanston and emptied out into Chicago, bordering the lakefront. I loved saying I lived on an L-shaped street. Maybe that's where my love for letters was born, living on the forearm of those two perpendicular lines, the L bent like an elbow, holding me close to the heart of my life.

Elizabeth and I spent a lot of time at Garden Park, that little meadow dotted with trees and playground equipment on the corner, flaring out from the joint of the L, overlooking the lake. You let us go there unsupervised—you let us go a lot of places unsupervised—and we often had the place to ourselves. We spent a lot of time just sitting in the grass, making necklaces out of rusty clover flowers, prying open damp, furry dandelion buds, sucking the sour milk from dandelion stems. We peered at the ladybugs, mating by the hundreds in the stone basin of the water fountain, a writhing mass of red and black. We stood in the pebbly picnic area overlooking the lake and watched the waves roll toward us. We smushed the poisonous-looking berries that grew on vines along the back fence and thrilled at the bitter, illicit scent they left on our fingers. We picked the violets that also grew along the back of the park and often came home with little bouquets for you, limp from the heat of our hands.

We invented a special game in front of our building. We each stood in one of the little patios that flanked the sunken entrance-way, then pointed to each other and yelled, "That's my house!" We'd run down the little steps and across the concrete to the opposite patio, giggling as we passed each other. Then we'd run up the steps of that patio, turn around, look at each other, point, yell, "That's my house!" and we'd run back again. This would continue, back and forth, back and forth, until we were too exhausted to go on.

When we were little, we were each other's house. We were each other's everything.

After we moved away from the building, after you finally convinced Dad to buy the house in Winnetka, the house I came to hate, the house where our family fell apart, the game got more subtle, more insidious. We didn't even realize we were playing it. Elizabeth wanted to inhabit my illness. I wanted to inhabit her long legs. She wanted my curly hair; I wanted her golden highlights. We wanted to move into each other's bodies—"That's my house," "That's my house." We used to be so comfortable with one another's bodies, but now even our own bodies had become foreign, volcanoes spewing over a once familiar landscape.

As soon as I traded in the "sick girl" mantle, Elizabeth readily picked it up. She began vomiting. Projectile vomiting, like something from *The Exorcist*. She would open her mouth during dinner and a huge firehose of puke would spray across the table and splat against the opposite wall. It was quite impressive. It was even more impressive when I learned years later that she was making herself do it—no finger down the throat, no syrup of ipecac; just sheer force of mind willing her body to empty itself.

When we went to visit Elizabeth at Children's Hospital, she wouldn't look at us. She lay on her side, facing away, a nasogastric tube up her nose, her spine as distinct as a string of pearls through her night shirt. I couldn't look at that elegant backbone, couldn't believe that long skinny girl was my little sister.

Her doctor had a crush on her. "She's looking more and more like Nastassja Kinski," he sighed. "Her eyes just keep getting bigger and bigger."

I felt a stab of jealousy. No one thought I looked like a glamorous movie star when I was sick. I was told my arms looked like Popsicle sticks. I was told my face looked like the moon.

You just couldn't see what was really happening with your girls.

"It's an eating disorder," one of Elizabeth's doctors said.

You denied it.

"She's doing it on purpose," one of her doctors said.

You denied it.

He put her on behavior modification therapy. One privilege was taken away after another: first the TV, then the phone, then objects from home, then friends weren't allowed to visit, then family. But she kept throwing up. And her body began to fall away, too. One thing after another was leaving her.

In the myth of Inanna, the goddess hears her sister moaning in the underworld. Inanna goes down to join her. At each gateway to the underworld, Inanna has to let go of another thing: at the first gate, her crown; at the second, her lapis beads; at the third, her sparkling stones; the fourth, her breastplate; the fifth, her gold ring; the sixth, her lapis divining rod; the seventh, her royal robe.

"You're killing her," you told the doctors.

"She's killing herself," they said in return.

Elizabeth didn't say a word. She was Inanna. She had to enter the underworld naked and unarmed. It was the only way she could approach her sister's throne.

NOVEMBER 28, 2009

When a person is missing, it's hard to know what to do. When a person is missing, you can search or you can wait, wait for the police to do their job, wait to hear from the missing person, a phone call, her voice saying something like, "I've been in Santa Barbara," or, "I've been wandering around Kmart. Why were you so worried?"

I find it hard to do much active searching with a newborn in my arms, but I do check the map around the Sherman Oaks Hospital, trying to imagine where she might have gone. The neighborhood seems to be mostly residential, but there's a War Memorial Park with a pool—could she have gone swimming? She didn't learn to swim until she was forty, but has become a nearly-every-day lap swimmer; she doesn't feel right if she doesn't get her swim in, she says. Michael goes through my mom's phone and calls all the people with a 760 area code, people he imagines might be friends, although she has very few friends, maybe no friends at this point. No one knows where she is; few have heard from her in months. My sister makes her own phone calls—hospitals; morgues. No sign anywhere.

"Why are you putting so much energy into this?" Hannah asks. "She's a grown woman."

"She's not in her right mind," I start, but then Elizabeth and I look at each other and take a deep breath. Maybe Hannah's right. Maybe we should relax a bit, not let our mom hijack our entire day. Maybe we should try to enjoy settling in with Asher, so warm in my arms.

I tell myself to stay off the computer the rest of the day, to focus on the people around me. I tell myself to try to not worry. To trust the police will find her.

·   ·   ·   ·

As evening falls, I feel a deep tug to check my e-mail. It feels important, necessary—my body wants to do it as fiercely as it wanted to push Asher out into the world. I excuse myself and log on to Gmail. Below a stack of requests for year-end donations, I find an e-mail sent five hours ago with the subject line "Your Mom" from someone named Duke Bristow. I open it, blood zipping. It reads:

> Your mother came by our house in Sherman Oaks and asked me to take her to union station which i did. I dropped her here and have parked, now looking for her.
>
> She spoke of you and your new baby and did not want to bother you today.
>
> I am concerned since if this was my mother and the roles were reversed I would want you to contact me.
>
> She says she has money, she has no luggage and no planned destination.
>
> Duke K. Bristow, Ph.D.

I kick myself for staying off the computer for so long. If I had found this sooner, I could have told the police to check Union Station. We could have found her hours ago. Now she could be anywhere a train could take her. I immediately write back and leave my number, then search for Duke Bristow online. I learn he is an associate professor of clinical finance and business economics at the USC Marshall School of Business. Had my mom sought him out for his financial expertise? Did she think he could help her find the millions she thought Dad was hiding?

I share the e-mail with my family.

"I had a feeling about Union Station," says Michael, and I don't doubt it. He can be eerily perceptive. "I should have said something."

I notice a phone number at the bottom of his e-mail; I don't have to wait for Duke Bristow to call—I can call him, myself. When

I do, Duke tells me my mom showed up in his front yard as he was mowing the lawn. She said she was the victim of domestic violence and needed to find a safe house. She asked for a ride to the train station. She was carrying a lot of money.

"How much?" I ask him.

"A lot," he says and leaves it at that. I worry—will someone find out and try to mug her? How much money is she actually carrying? Where did it come from? I picture her with a briefcase full of cash, like the kind people use to pay a ransom in the movies, stacks of crisp bills banded together. A thought flashes through my mind—*maybe she found the motherlode she's been searching for*—before I shake it away.

"She thinks my dad is hiding millions of dollars from her," I tell him. "She's not really being abused."

He seems stunned. "She's very elegant," he tells me. He tells me how proud she is of me—he was able to find me because she told him about my novels and he contacted me through my website—how proud she is of the new baby. He tells me she said, "Asher Whitman Brandeis" sounds like the name of a Nobel laureate or a Supreme Court justice. She has great ambitions for her new grandson. I don't know whether to laugh or cry.

Duke Bristow offers to be of assistance in any way he can. I give him the name and number of the police officer I spoke to; I give him her case number. He promises to call.

My mom thinks everyone is out to get her, that everyone is against her, but everyone we talk to only wants to help, only wants to get her home, safe. I wish she could know this, could somehow feel it in her bones. I try to feel her in my own bones, try to imagine how she must be feeling right now. She must be so scared; she must feel so alone. I dip my nose onto Asher's head and take a deep whiff of his scalp. The top of a baby's head is like a sedative, the sweetest drug I know. I take another deep draught of it and try to imagine sending its calming power to my mom, wherever she may be.

[Cut to a closeup of paintings, the crack between them.]

ARLENE: I think this painting just shows the
disorientation I felt. I felt I was just going down
the rabbit hole and the whole world seemed to just go
mad, and then finally I said, "We have to take her out
of this hospital; they're going to kill this child if
we don't take her out," and we moved her to another
hospital, and she was in terrible shape. She had lost
an enormous amount of weight; she was in a wheelchair
because all of her muscle mass was gone, and her hip,
because of the Ehlers-Danlos, couldn't hold the bone
in its socket, so she couldn't walk. So she went into
the hospital walking and in really good nutritional
shape and left there like they created an eating
disorder for her. So it was maddening. It was the most
horrific experience of my life.

Mom,

I would often find you sitting in the living room with a glass of Scotch when Elizabeth was in the hospital. You would just sit there, frozen, not acknowledging me, completely zoned out. I had never seen you drink Scotch before this; you were always a Chardonnay kind of woman, and only at restaurants, at dinner. This was the middle of the day. I started to wonder if you had done this when I was in the hospital, too. I had pictured you always busy with your mother-of-the-sick-girl quests, research spurred on by a sense of purpose. I hadn't pictured this—you sitting with a glass of Scotch, stony-faced, wanting to disappear. I had always thought my illness was a moment of glory for you, a shining moment for us both, a chance for you to gleam with righteous anger.

One day, you were late picking me up after school. I waited at the curb for over an hour, telling myself that if three red cars went past, it meant you had died. Three red cars went past, and I told myself that three more red cars had to go past for it to be real. One red car, then two . . . I told myself that if four blue cars went past, I should start walking home. Four blue cars came and went, and you still weren't there, but I didn't move; I didn't start walking; I wasn't sure if I wanted you to be alive or dead, wasn't sure if I wanted you to come or not. I started to cry, but I wasn't sure why. Finally, you careened up to the curb. You didn't apologize. Your breath smelled fruity. I told you that; I said, "Your breath smells fruity." You didn't say anything. You just drove me home, seething, as if I had done something wrong by standing on the curb, counting cars, imagining your death. I found myself getting mad, too, as we drove home, more and more mad, but I didn't say anything. Neither of us said a word. We got home and you went straight up to your bedroom, and I tried to think of the most destructive thing I could do. I decided

I would huff some nitrous oxide. I had never done it before, but there was a can of whipped cream in the fridge. I had heard that if you pressed the tip in a certain way, the nitrous would come out. I tried; I sucked in sweetened air. I tried again; more sweet air. No effect. I didn't know anything. I didn't even know how to get high. I squirted a mountain of whipped cream into my mouth instead, and let it melt slowly on my tongue, the extent of my rebellion.

When I was sick, Elizabeth ran away. Her best friend had moved to New Jersey. Elizabeth stole your credit card, took a cab to the airport, got on a People's Express flight to New York, back when you could buy a ticket right on the plane, and took off. No one questioned her. She was ten years old. You tracked her down via your credit card company, had our brother Jon, who lived in New York, meet her as she got off the plane. You ended up letting her get on another flight to New Jersey. She had been through a lot while I was sick; she deserved to see her best friend.

She had chutzpah; you had wine breath; I had a mouthful of whipped cream, dissolving into nothing.

NOVEMBER 29, 2009

None of us sleep much. We aren't sure what to do with ourselves in the morning. The police don't have any updates. Elizabeth walks to the children's bookstore downtown to get a gift for Michael's nephew, who turns eight today; Michael's sister and both boys are coming over later to meet Asher. Michael wonders if he should go to Union Station to do his own sleuthing before their visit. After Elizabeth returns with a gift-wrapped book, an unfamiliar number with a 213 area code calls. My pulse is strong in my ears as I flip open my phone.

"Congratulations! I hear you had a baby!" a man's voice booms, hearty and jolly; his accent is strong but I can't place it.

"Thank you," I say hesitantly. "Who is this?" I wonder if it's a telemarketer trying to sell subscription diaper service or life insurance or baby portrait packages.

"My name is Pablo Paschal," he says. "I have your mother."

"Oh, thank God," I blurt, heart surging, even though I don't believe in a traditional God, even though there's something slightly sinister in "I have your mother." Had he kidnapped her? Could all her money be some sort of ransom, after all? "Is she okay?" I ask.

"She is fine," he says, "but you need to love and support her. You need to say 'You can sleep on my couch, Mommy.'" For this last part, he makes his voice sound high, like a little girl's. Like how he thinks I should sound.

A stranger has called to make me feel even more guilty, even more like a bad daughter?

"Can I talk to her?" I ask. I can hear her in the background, but can't tell what she's saying.

"I'll put her on speaker phone," he says.

"Hello, Gayle." Her voice is cold. She only calls me "Gayle" if she's mad at me—otherwise, it's *Gayley* or *honey*. I dissolve into tears, anyway.

"Oh Mom, oh Mom," I weep. "I'm so glad you're okay. We've been so worried."

Elizabeth and Michael stand nearby, on edge, waiting.

"You should be worried," she says. "I'm in grave danger."

I hear Pablo Paschal in the background, saying, "Remember, be positive. Be positive."

"Where are you?" I ask, and that's how I learn that my Jewish mother has gone to La Placita, Our Lady Queen of Angels, the oldest church in Los Angeles, for sanctuary. It's right near Union Station, on historic Olvera Street, the "Birthplace of Los Angeles." She didn't get on a train at all; she just walked across the street. Had she slept there last night? The man who called me is Father Paschal, it turns out, not Pablo Paschal.

"She's at a church in LA," I whisper to my family and watch their eyebrows lift.

"Tell her I'll go get her," Elizabeth whispers back.

My mom launches into her spiel about being followed, being poisoned, about Dad being behind it, all things I've heard before, all things she can't seem to stop herself from saying. In the background, Father Paschal says, "Find a positive solution, Mom. Find a positive solution." As a result, she slows down her voice but says the same exact thing. "I know it sounds fanciful," she says again, this time with all the vowels drawn out, her voice deeper than usual, as if a tape of her normal voice has been slowed, and again I wish for fanciful, for unicorns, for fairies dancing from flower to flower. This isn't fanciful. This is excruciating. She tells me that in the hospital, a Middle Eastern couple had been staring at her, that the woman had sprayed poison at her with her cell phone; that's why my mom had ripped out her IVs; that's why she left without telling anyone. But now she's found a safe place. Father Paschal has been nothing but kind.

"I'm so glad," I tell her. "Stay there. Elizabeth will come get you. We love you so much."

·   ·   ·   ·

Elizabeth calls Sandra, our mom's therapist, who helps arrange for a psychiatric evaluation team to meet her and our mom at La Placita. If Sandra hadn't seen our mom's delusions before, she sure sees them now. As Elizabeth gets ready to take off, the air feels tense, charged, like she's leaving for war; we hug as if we're never going to see each other again.

I hope La Placita is keeping our mom placid for the time being. I assume Placita means "the most peaceful," which seems both perfect and completely ironic, but when I look it up, I learn it means "plaza," "marketplace," "public square," pretty much the opposite of peaceful.

About an hour later, I get a call—Elizabeth is lost. Downtown LA is confusing, especially where the 10, 110, and 101 freeways converge. I try to give her directions, but my brain feels scrambled; I'm not able to offer the best advice. She phones again a while later, still lost, starting to get frantic. While we're talking, a call waiting beep comes from our mom. I tell Elizabeth I'll call her right back.

"Gayle." My mom's voice shakes with anger. "Are you planning to put me on a twenty-four-hour hold?"

"No," I say, my own voice starting to tremble. It's not a lie, this "No." We ideally want her to be held much longer than twenty-four hours.

"You can't do this to me!" she yells. "I have a plan! I need to get my case together!"

"Mom," I start, but I don't know what to say.

"You can't do this to me," she yells again.

"Mom," I say, "we just want you to get the help you need." As soon as it comes out of my mouth, I regret it. I've always had trouble being honest with my mom—why in the world would I blurt out the truth now?

"For once in your life, give me the benefit of the doubt," she cries, her voice getting higher and higher. "For once in your LIFE!"

· · · ·

The phone goes dead. I try to call back, but there's no answer.

A few minutes later, Elizabeth calls; she's talked to Father Paschal. Our mom has taken off, running down Cesar Chavez Ave. She ran so fast, the priest, much younger than her, wasn't able to catch up.

"I see an exit for Cesar Chavez," she says. "Should I take it?"

"I don't know," I tell her. "It's a pretty long street—I don't think the exit is close to the church."

My heart is hammering. What have I done?

Elizabeth gets to La Placita around the same time as the two women Sandra had arranged to do the psychiatric evaluation. Ten minutes after our mom ran away.

ARLENE: It turned out after the second hospital, they
    realized, they said especially with a diagnosis
    of Ehlers-Danlos, that they never should have done
    that to her, treated her for an eating disorder,
    so fortunately she was in a good place, she had a
    wonderful woman gastroenterologist, a woman who sent
    her home with a gastric feeding tube that she put
    down her own nose every night—this twelve-year-old
    kid hooked herself up to this pump and this liquid
    nourishment and managed it until it stopped, and she
    called me at work one day and said, "I had breakfast
    and it stayed down—will you come home?" And of
    course I just tore out of there and went home,
    and it stopped.

Mom,

You drove me to the Old Orchard movie theater complex one night so I could meet my friends at the premiere of *The Breakfast Club*. The movie had been based on the early morning detention at my high school. John Hughes was there for an after-the-show panel discussion, as was Anthony Michael Hall and my potential movie-of-the-week alter ego, Ally Sheedy.

I got in your car after the movie all abuzz. I felt like I had just been part of something significant. You were silent the whole ride home as I rattled on and on about the ills of society and how we're really all the same under the surface, but our culture wants to separate us into all these cliques and blah blah blah. Finally, you came to a screeching halt at a stoplight by the White Hen Pantry and turned to me.

"Your sister might be dying," you said, your voice icy. "And you're talking about society?! Your sister's vitals are dropping, and you're worried about our culture? Get your priorities straight, Gayle!"

I hadn't ever entertained the possibility that Elizabeth might really die. I felt like a knife had been plunged into my stomach.

A thought entered my mind: *If she does die, she'll die innocent, pure. She won't ever have to deal with the seamier side of life.* I felt guilty thinking that, but part of me meant it. I didn't want to grow up and I didn't want her—the purest link to my own childhood—to grow up, either. She had been in such a hurry to get older, to seem older, and I was strangely grateful her illness had put the brakes on that for a while. If she was in the hospital, she couldn't smoke cigarettes or drink wine coolers or wear makeup or make out with boys or run away. And I would have witnessed her whole life. Her whole pure and innocent life.

．　．　．　．

The fact that Elizabeth didn't die makes me want to kiss each inch of the ground in gratitude. I can't imagine being on this planet without her.

Unlike me, she became more famous after her hospitalization than during it. She was skinny now; she became instantly popular, embraced by the girls in her eighth-grade class at Washburne who had shunned her before. Our lives barely intersected once she returned.

When we were younger, we lived in the bubble of our collective imagination. We lived in that bubble right until my illness began. Once we started creating our own illnesses, we stopped creating shared worlds.

NOVEMBER 29, 2009

Elizabeth calls me back as she waits for police to arrive. The women Sandra had sent were both very kind—one had peeling orange nail polish and a smoker's voice, Elizabeth tells me; she seems like she's had a rough life but has pulled it together. The other mostly did paperwork. Father Paschal is a beautiful, moon-faced Nigerian man, Elizabeth says, and I feel a sudden pang that I don't get to meet this cast of characters with her. I haven't been out of the house since Asher was born; I don't feel capable of being out in the world yet, my body still aching and leaking, but I long to be there with my sister, to try to find our mom together.

Our mom had left a note for Father Paschal to give to us. Elizabeth reads it to me:

> Gayle and Elizabeth, For once in your lives, give me a 30 day benefit of the doubt.

My heart sinks. The very words my mom had yelled at me; the very words burned into my brain—"For once in your LIFE!"—were not as impulsive, as passionate as they had seemed. They were part of her script. Either that, or the letter is a continuation of that conversation, but she left so quickly, she must have written it before she called.

Elizabeth continues reading; it feels strange to hear our mom's words in my sister's voice, which she manages to keep remarkably calm and steady.

> *I know this all appears unbelievable, but it is not.*
> *I left my car at the hospital Friday night where I went with chest pains, given blood thinners, the under the tongue medication, blood tests and heart monitoring. The Sherman Oaks Hospital*

on Van Nuys, in Van Nuys, where the 101 merges with (near) the 405. All was going well at the hospital until a Middle Eastern couple, appearing to visit across the hall, seemed to watch only me. After breakfast, I felt the same reaction to whatever Dad sprayed onto me. The woman, not an employee, came in to ask how I feel. She seemed surprised I appeared to be doing well. Drinking large amounts of fluids helps. It occurred to me I would be left in a permanent state like that drug induced condition if I did not leave, if I were released to this couple. Find out who they are and why they were permitted access to me?

My car is full of fast food stuff, my computers, my project's original film and external ports. My project is completely gone without that. Feeling safe again is the only concern right now. I always am surrounded by Middle Eastern men, in flat bed trucks, hotel rooms (wall apart), on buses and stores. The spray seems to come from a high tech phone and makes a ping sound when it goes off. Some of the same license plates are 8W87425—white Titan, 8A01957 Red flat bed truck and SUV 6V12067. The first two followed me from La Jolla to Coronado to Santa Barbara and left when I pulled into the emergency room, between Thurs and Sat. I have asked some of these men why they follow me. Two said "You will be caught." Others deny any contact. I don't know what if any trumped up charges were being cooked up. Ask at the hospital and especially why they (the couple) were given access to me. At the last hotel to be given safe escort from my hotel to my car, I asked hotel management to call police. The police did not write a report and gave me the wrong address to the Enlightenment Fellowship Retreat. Many of those men at that hotel were white, not Middle Eastern.

You can get my license # from Hyundai in Carlsbad's service department.

I still need to find a safe house, the one in Irvine I was headed to on Thursday did not answer their phone when I got close.

Call to cancel Maria [number]

Sandra Wed. 5:00 [number]

Sarita [number]

Ask Adam Lansky, sound editor [number] and Frank Quattrocci [number] if my project is or ever will be complete?

I know how baazar [sic] this seems, but just give me 30 days to try to work this out.

Give the beautiful baby boy a big kiss from me. Tell Michael how appalled I am that he asked me to leave like that, in front of my grandchildren. Your golden husband is badly tarnished.

Sarita may have my key (house). DO NOT let your father have access to my home.

The things I need most—all vitamins and Jenuvia [sic] samples, cabinet and bottom drawer to the left of the stove. Diabetes testing equipment in the back bathroom, bottom shelf next to the toilet. The Sherman Oaks Hospital still has my medication and vitamins in their pharmacy.

Please—Please—Please work with me here for the next 30 to 45 days.

Mom

CINDY LAUREN, executive director, Ehlers-Danlos National
Foundation: There's a human truism that we all like
stories, so me quoting facts and statistics is like
"ugh." (Closes eyes and throws back head and hand) But
your story, or her story, is going to engage someone's
attention, and they're going to remember when that
next patient walks through the door and this weird
constellation of symptoms that doesn't seem to fit;
it's not nothing, but it's not the biggies—cancer,
diabetes, or MS—it's something, and what we're looking
to do . . . is asking physicians to stop for a minute—
hmmm, maybe I should consider this.

Mom,

One night when I was sixteen, we were on our way out to dinner. Dad was driving the Park Avenue while you were in the passenger seat, sealed in your own thoughts. Now that both your daughters were well, you seemed a bit lost. You were drinking less, but you didn't seem to know what to do with your time. Years later, you would sue Elizabeth's doctors, would force her to fly home from college and sit through a trial where she couldn't bring herself to tell the truth about making herself throw up, but we weren't there yet.

I had my Walkman clamped over my ears, my eyes closed, head tipped back against the plush burgundy seat. I was thinking about being in the backseat of another car, with my first serious boyfriend; we had parked behind a theological seminary the night before, Howard Jones crooning, "Don't always look at the rain . . ."

Elizabeth must have known. After weeks, months, years of barely touching, I could feel her reach across the gap between us. I could feel her hand hover over my face, could smell the corn-chip dust on her palm. She must have known I was thinking about a kiss. She laid two fingers across my lips—her index finger, her middle finger; she laid them lightly across my lips like she wanted to take me back to that other backseat.

I opened my eyes, startled. She lifted her fingers from my mouth and looked right at me. Her eyes healthy. Her eyes not shadowed by dark circles, her eyes not bloodshot, her eyelids not heavy and oily looking. Her healthy eyes looking into my healthy eyes. Both of us healthy together. Both of us healthy and looking at each other and not sure what to do next. It had been so long since we had known what to do.

.   .   .   .

After I went off to college, Elizabeth and I found each other again, found fierce, sweet reconnection. The first time she came out to visit me on her own, we tried to concoct a way for her to stay a while longer. The only way we could change her ticket without penalties, we learned, was to get a doctor's note to prove she had been too sick to fly. We spent our extra day together driving from one clinic to another, looking for a doctor who would write us this note. She pretended to have flu, she pretended to have a sore throat, she pretended to be constipated, to have trouble peeing. No one would believe her. We found this hysterical. Neither of us had admitted to having fabricated illness at this point—our confessions would come several years down the road—but we knew. We knew we had been the divas of disease, the starlets of sickness. The sick girls who were now girls glowing with health. Girls who, for the blessed, blessed life of us, couldn't convince anyone we were anything other than well.

NOVEMBER 29, 2009

Elizabeth ends up riding around downtown LA in the back of a police car with two cops: a fresh faced rookie, and a burly guy who seems scary at first, but is respectful to everyone he meets—from a homeless woman they encounter to the doorman at the fancy hotel where our mom had spent the night. The police had checked our mom's credit card records and learned she had stayed at the Kyoto Grand, where she had checked in under the name Ann Brand, similar to a pseudonym she's used before. I wonder what sort of life she imagined for Ann Brand, wonder if she's still using the name now.

Michael's sister and her two sons are due soon. I'm not sure I'm up for a visit, given my general state of deshabille and panic, but it seems unsociable to tell them not to come. And we have a present, thanks to Elizabeth. I don't know what we'd do without her.

Michael takes Asher so I can slog off to the shower; each step feels like pulling my feet through mud, like my body is full of lead. My breasts are rock hard with milk and aching; my right armpit is, too, some breast tissue having migrated there. If I sliced my swollen armpit open, would milk come gushing out?

Once the water starts to pour over me, I feel lighter. I feel myself dissolving into steam, milk flowing down my body, my edges blurring, mind emptying. Bliss. I stay under the shower head until my skin is poached pink, until the hot water runs out and goosebumps prickle me back into my body and my arms start to ache for Asher again.

My hair is still wet when Mette and the boys arrive. They are instantly enamored with Asher and take turns holding him on the couch. I worry they won't remember to support Asher's head, but of course, they do fine; they are utterly responsible and charming and careful.

I feel myself on the verge of hysteria. As soon as Mette asks about my mom, I burst into tears.

"Let me know if I can help," she says. "I know what it's like to have to go looking for your mom." She rolls her eyes and gives a little laugh.

Mette and Michael's mom has had issues with substance abuse—prescription pain medication. She has disappeared at times, too, once after her live-in boyfriend was arrested for parole violation. Her kids sent her back to Denmark a few years ago because her addiction had gotten out of control; they thought she'd have a better chance of getting clean at home. It seems to have worked. She moved back to the States last year; she stayed with us for a couple of tense weeks until we found a subsidized apartment that would take half of her $447 monthly Social Security check. Jette is a difficult woman—racist, intolerant, snippy, judgmental. Whoever says Denmark has the happiest people in the world has not met this sour puss. She makes me miss my former mother-in-law all the more deeply.

"Are you doing anything special for your birthday?" I try to sound like a normal person as I talk to the birthday boy, try to sound like my body isn't a grenade of milk and anxiety. He doesn't seem to notice I am holding on by a thread; he shrugs and smiles at me shyly with his big, gorgeous eyes. Both boys are beautiful; if Asher grows to look anything like them—or anything like his own siblings, for that matter—he'll be a stunner.

"We were thinking of finding a movie," says Mette.

"I'll check the listings," I say, suddenly eager to have the house back to ourselves. I want to be able to take off my shirt and sob without scaring anyone. I find a kid-friendly movie starting at 4:45; it's 4:50 now. "It's right down the street," I tell her. "With all the previews, I doubt you'll miss a thing."

. . . .

After our guests leave, I check my e-mail again. I have been keeping Duke Bristow up to date about my mom's whereabouts; when
I told him she was at La Placita earlier today and my sister was
on her way there, he was so relieved. "Your mother seems to have
an angel looking out for her," he wrote. I suddenly remember my
mom telling me that she had once tried to gas herself in the garage, back in 1994. She said the ghost of her mom had pushed
her out of the car just as the world started to fade. And another
time, she said that she had taken too much Tylenol—an inten-
tional overdose?—and when she looked in the mirror, she saw her
mother's face, the way she looked when she had died, and that's
when she knew she needed to get her stomach pumped. Stories I
never fully believed; stories that didn't get the response from me
she had been hoping for. Duke Bristow now knows she has run
away. "Please tell me if you successfully recover her," he writes. "It
seems you are very close."

DEATH AND TRANSFIGURATION .

ARLENE: This painting is called *Death and Transfiguration*,
and I call it my family portrait. It's about all of
the deaths in my family. The first one, as you can
see, is not connected to the bloodline—um, that was
a friend of mine, who died back in 1965 [she doesn't
say this was her sister's psychiatrist, Eli], but all
the others are my brothers and one sister who died, in
the order in which they died. The G is for my mother,
Gertrude; the B for my father, Benjamin. So it's a
pretty sad family history. My brother Harvey, the first
one to die, in 1970, was forty-two, and then Leonard
was forty-five (starts to cry). Al was forty-eight,
Sheldon was fifty-one; Louis, my oldest brother, was
sixty when he died; Don was sixty-five, and Rochelle
was sixty-five. The family history is so profound that
I think it's a story that has to be told, not just
because it's my family but because of lots of people's
families, who are dealing with this, who don't know

126

what they're dealing with, who really need help in
dealing with their doctors, and I think it's crucial
to pay attention to these spirits that came to me to
tell this story, and it's, I think it's the hour of
the moment of my life to be able to do this (nodding,
closing her eyes as she cries some more).

Mom,

When I did my study abroad in Bali my senior year at the University of Redlands, I ended up with a bad case of Bali Belly.

I blamed the fruit ices. They had been so refreshing, those glittering mounds of mango and passion fruit and papaya snow. They had been so artfully arranged in their large glass bowl, decorated with spears of pineapple and sprigs of mint. I neglected to ask whether the water for the ice had been boiled, whether the fruit had been soaked in bleach. I don't know why I had overlooked it; I loved the word for boiled—*rebus*. I loved the word for water—*air*. I was paying the price for being so remiss with my words. Now my language training was expanding to include words like *sakit perut* (stomach ache), *kentut* (fart), and *bau* (bad smell).

I was on the Indonesian island to study the local dance and music; my eyes and wrists had grown more flexible while learning the graceful, twitchy pendet, a dance of greeting, of offering; my ears had acclimated themselves to the jangly gamelan instruments. I had fallen in love with the green terraced rice fields, and the cheeky monkeys, and the women holding towers of fruit and flowers on their heads, and the tempeh satay with peanut sauce. It was my final semester of college at the University of Redlands; I had chosen to travel to the island for my study abroad with a group from the Naropa Institute, a Tibetan Buddhist college out of Boulder, Colorado. For about a week, while most of the group began their day with sitting meditation, I began (and filled and ended) my day squatting over the pit toilet in my outdoor bathroom.

I shared a stone bungalow with three women—my roommate Celia was a healer; next door were Rebecca, an herbalist and former midwife, and Angela, a nurse. If I had to be sick in Bali, at least I was surrounded by the right people.

While the rest of the group attended a cremation ceremony, Angela stayed behind to act as my guardian angel. Every time I stumbled out of the bathroom, or drifted out of sleep, I found a small gift on my bed stand—a fresh bottle of Sprite, a sprig of flowers, a bendy straw, a mini Paddington bear clipped to the handle of a mug. Rebecca—who, to my continual amazement, had one brown eye and one half-brown, half-blue, split down the center—introduced me to the pleasures and healthful properties of ginger root tea. And Celia saved me.

One day, when I was feeling feverish and fretful, she climbed inside the mosquito netting around my bed and knelt beside me. Light poured through the window cut into the stone wall, filling her curly hair with fire. The air was humid as a mouth. She put one hand flat on my stomach. I flinched.

"You're carrying a lot of pain in there," she said, her British accent an instant balm.

"I was sick as a teenager," I told her, blinking back tears. I watched a lizard climb through the window, skitter across the wall. "I spent a lot of time in the hospital."

"For what?" she asked. I could feel heat pour from her hand, through my shirt, through my skin.

"They thought it was Crohn's disease, but that was probably wrong. I found out a couple of years ago that I have porphyria. . . ."

I didn't tell her about my year of pretending to be ill. I hadn't told anyone yet. It was my deepest, darkest secret.

"You have a lot to release," Celia said. I really started crying then, but she continued, her voice as calm as ever. "I know you'll probably want to have a baby someday, and you won't want to have so much negative energy stored up in your belly. The baby wouldn't like that."

I nodded, sniffling. My period was a week late at that point, but I hadn't said anything, hadn't been ready to confront my own suspicions. I would find out a week later that I was pregnant with Arin, the same day your sister, Rochelle, told you she had a dream that I was going to have a baby.

"I'm going to lift my hand," she said, "And I want all the bad stuff in your belly to lift up with it. You don't need it anymore. Let it go and trust in your body's ability to heal itself."

I closed my eyes. I felt her hand rise from my stomach. My diaphragm bounced like a trampoline. I felt a space open near my solar plexus. I felt the pain and shame of those earlier years begin to dribble out, then stream, then shoot into the monsoonal air like a sprinkler, a geyser, a fine gray spray.

RE: SEARCH II

Diagnosing Myself

MALINGERING
ma·lin·ger
/mə'liNGgər/

verb
gerund or present participle: **malingering**

exaggerate or feign illness in order to escape duty or work.
synonyms: pretend to be ill, feign (an) illness, fake (an) illness; shirk; informal: goof off

"he was put on report for malingering"

I didn't hear the term malingering until I was in my thirties, or if I had heard it, I probably thought it meant something like "loitering." As soon as a friend mentioned that a professor had accused her of malingering during a year when she was frequently ill, I looked up the definition and felt a shock of recognition. That's what I was, I thought: a malingerer. It felt strange to know I had fit a pattern, a diagnosis, that this shameful secret, this weirdness that had seemed so unique to my family, had a clear, solid name. If I had been given this diagnosis when I was in the midst of my prolonged teenage illness, I would have been aghast. As a Latin student, I knew "mal" meant "bad," so I would have inferred that "malingering" meant lingering in the bad. I never wanted to be associated with the word "bad" in any way at that age. Of course I knew illness itself was de facto bad, but being the sick girl had somehow bathed me in a pallid glow that could so easily pass for goodness.

FACTITIOUS DISORDER
fac·ti·tious
/fak'tiSHəs/

adjective
artificially created or developed. "a largely factitious national identity"

dis·or·der
/dis'ôrdər/

noun
1. **a state of confusion.** "tiresome days of mess and disorder"
2. **a disruption of normal physical or mental functions; a disease or abnormal condition.** "eating disorders"

Just recently, I looked up "malingering" again and learned it wasn't the correct diagnosis, after all. To malinger, one must be in search of material gain—the woman who pretends to have cancer so she can raise money on GoFundMe, the soldier who exaggerates (or self-inflicts) injury to earn medals or honorable discharge. A much more accurate term exists: "factitious disorder." I like this name better. It's a good diagnosis for a writer, like another name for creative nonfiction.

Unlike a malingerer, a person with a factitious disorder desires to occupy the sick role itself, and the emotional—not material—boons that come with it. In their study "Factitious Disease: Clinical Lessons from Case Studies at Baylor University Medical Center," Adria C. Savino and John S. Fordtran, MD, note "the main tangible emotional gains that patients receive from assuming the sick role are believed to be sympathy, warmth, and nurturance; a heroic image for tolerating illness so bravely; relief from an expected achiever role; and control over their lives." Check, check, check, check, check, check.

The term "factitious disease" was coined in 1843 in *On Feigned and Factitious Diseases Chiefly of Soldiers and Seamen, On the Means Used to Simulate or Produce Them and On the Best Modes of Discovering Impostors* by Hector Gavin, friend to Charles Dickens and Florence Nightingale. Gavin wasn't the first to note the phenomenon; Claudius Galen*, who some call the most influential medical writer in history, wrote his own treatise, *On Feigned Diseases and the Detection of Them*, way back in the second century.*

Gavin focused on men in the military in his study, but he noted that a number of women "assume the semblance of disease for some inexplicable cause"; today, more women than men are diagnosed with factitious disorder, by a 3:1 ratio. In a *Time* magazine interview, Dr. Marc Feldman, foremost authority on factitious disorders, referenced a feminist theory suggesting that "women are negated and their needs are frequently ignored and so some decide that the only way that they can get their needs met is by appearing to be ill."

For a malingerer, the production and motivation of the illness are both conscious acts; for someone with a factitious disorder, the production is conscious but the motivation is not. It took years for me to unravel my own motivations; I'm sure there are tangles yet to discover.

·   ·   ·

---

*My mom almost named me Gaylen, adding the G from her mom, Gertrude, to her maiden name, Baylen. I'm glad to not be saddled by that name, the name of a family wracked by mental illness, heart disease, silence; although of course I carry that family in half my DNA, in all my cells, that name written into my body whether I like it or not. I don't think my mom knew of Galen when she was considering the name, couldn't have envisioned that her daughter would one day come to embody Galen's observations.

It's strange, even now, to see myself as a textbook case; I had thought I was creating something brand new—a feat of simultaneous self-manufacture and self-erasure—never guessing other girls were doing the same. My mom had raised me and my sister to believe we were special snowflakes, but we were part of a flurry of factitious sick girls, a flurry invisible to us, dazzled as we were by our own crystalline structure. Even my methods were textbook—surreptitious laxative use is quite common among girls and women with factitious disorders, it turns out, although so are other drastic measures. One article in the medical journal *Psychiatry*, "Munchausen's Syndrome and Other Factitious Disorders in Children Case Series and Literature Review," gives examples:

- a teenager who demanded and received pain medication for her nonexistent sickle cell disease.
- a thirteen-year-old girl with factitious hematuria and purpura with a three-year history of tampering with urine.
- a fourteen-year-old girl with factitious toenail infections and a three-year history of hydrofluoric acid use.
- a fifteen-year-old girl with factitious wrist edema/reflex sympathetic dystrophy and a six-month history of tourniquet use.
- a sixteen-year-old girl with factitious proteinuria and pain and a three-year history of injecting raw eggs into her bladder.
- an eighteen-year-old girl with subcutaneous emphysema, tongue ulcers, dermatitis autogenica, and a nine-month history of injection of air under her skin.
- a fifteen-year-old girl with factitious panniculitis and a three-month history of milk injections.
- a fifteen-year-old girl with factitious systemic lupus and a history of coloring her face with paint.

No one can say we factitious sick girls aren't creative. An article from Baylor University Medical Center Proceedings states, "The type of illness feigned or produced is limited only by the patient's medical knowledge and creativity."

In her memoir, *Lying*, Lauren Slater discusses how she developed Munchausen syndrome—the most serious and chronic form of factitious disorder—at thirteen. "Perhaps I was, and still am, a pretender," she writes, "a person who creates illness because she needs time, attention, touch, because she knows no other way of telling her life's tale."

RE: SEARCH III

More Postmortem Diagnosis

ANOSOGNOSIA

ano · sog · no · sia

\‚a-nō-‚säg-'nō-zh(ē-)ə\

noun

medical

: an inability or refusal to recognize a defect or disorder that is
clinically evident

> *Mrs. M.'s form of anosognosia is even more extreme: she not only
> flatly denies she is paralyzed, she refuses to admit that the limp
> limb on the left has anything at all to do with her.*
>
> —James Shreeve, *Discover*, May 1995

> *A prominent feature of schizophrenia and bipolar disorder is
> anosognosia, a sick person's unawareness that he is sick.*
>
> —Algis Valiunas, *New Atlantis*, Winter 2009
>
> —examples from Merriam-Webster's online dictionary

Another word I recently stumbled upon, a word that shed sudden
and startling light, is "anosognosia." The roots of the word are
Greek—*nosos* means disease, *gnosis*, knowledge (literally "to not
know a disease"). It's strange how I went to such lengths to insist I
was ill when I was not, and my mom insisted she was not ill when
she so acutely was. The inverse of one another, my yin to her yang.

Anosognosia affects half of all people with schizophrenia and 40 percent of all people with bipolar disorder. It is the main reason why many people with mental illness don't take their meds or are never diagnosed to begin with. The term has only been used in psychiatric applications since the 1980s, but it was coined by a French neurologist in 1914, and the condition has been acknowledged for centuries; in the 1604 play *The Honest Whore*, playwright Thomas Dekker wrote, "That proves you mad because you know it not."

Many mentally ill homeless people have anosognosia; many people who abscond from hospitals do, as well. Quite the opposite of people with factitious disorder, who go to outrageous lengths to be hospitalized.

Doctors used to think anosognosia was a protective factor against suicide—they imagined lack of awareness of illness meant psychotic people were less likely to develop suicidal ideation. Later studies showed this was not true; this was not true at all.

After he takes Hannah to school in the morning, Michael says, "I keep thinking about Pasadena. I think Arlene took a train to Pasadena." As perceptive as he is, I worry Michael can be too invested in his intuition, too fiercely certain of its messages. My mom is like that, too. She's convinced she's a "medical intuitive," and, in fact, when I was a kid and was supposed to have my tonsils out, she thought maybe it was allergies, and she was right; her intuition saved me from surgery.

My mom's mom escaped a tonsillectomy herself when she was a young woman in 1915. Her employers at Western Electric told her that if she didn't have her tonsils removed, she wouldn't be able to continue to work there. My grandmother was grateful for the job coiling telephone wire on an assembly line, but she didn't think it was worth going under the knife. She quit, which turned out to be a timely decision. Not long afterward, twenty-five hundred Western Electric employees and their families boarded the *Eastland* steamer on the Chicago River, headed out to Lake Michigan for a daylong cruise and company picnic. The boat tipped over while still in port, trapping passengers underwater, killing more than eight hundred. Maybe she was an intuitive, too. Maybe my mom and Elizabeth and I all owe our lives to that intuition; our kids, too. We follow up on Michael's hunch and talk to the Amtrak police again. No sightings to report.

Michael and Elizabeth decide to drive down to the Sherman Oaks Hospital and pick up our mom's car, her medicine, and her vitamins. This at least is something tangible we can do—or at least they can do. It will be my first time home alone with the baby— the thought fills me with anxiety. Asher looks so vulnerable in my arms, so fragile. What if I drop him? I may have raised two kids, but somehow feel as if I've never been alone with a baby in my life. The first time I was home alone with Arin nineteen years ago, he projectile vomited right after Matt left, and I ran outside in a panic in my nightgown to catch him before he drove away.

I talk to my dad over the phone as Michael and Elizabeth get ready to go. "I just want her home, in her own bed," he says, his voice breaking. "Even if she'll never see me again, I just want her home."

A call from a 213 area code beeps onto the line.

"I need to answer this" I tell my dad. "It could be the police."

"I'll wait," he says and I hand the phone to my sister so she can take the call.

She says, "Hello," and then something happens to her face, something I've never seen before. It's like watching a time lapse of weather patterns, the way color and emotion sweep across her face, a changing landscape of pale and flush, crumple and stretch. Michael says, "Oh, no," and all my bones dissolve even before Elizabeth drops to her knees. "It's the coroner's office," she says. "She's dead." Then again, louder, "She's dead!"

A space opens up in me. A vast white space.

I can't call it relief, not exactly. I can't call it calm. I can't call it numb, either. Calm implies something that can get stirred up. Numb implies something that can thaw.

This is different.

This is blank.

This is something nothing can touch.

A sea—white as milk, but not wet as milk—opens right at the center of me, where all my organs used to sit. An erasure of all that was once there. A void so blank, so white, one could almost mistake it for joy.

.   .   .   .

The older daughter splits in half. She hears weird guttural sounds coming out of her throat, but she doesn't feel them. Half of her has left her body, observes herself in grief. She turns to her husband, Michael—he is making strange sounds, too, his mouth twisted into a Mobius strip—it doesn't look real, his mouth, his pain. He is making similar sounds to her; she wonders if he is trying to sound like her, the way he sometimes does when they have sex, matching tone for tone. She wonders if he is trying to mirror her as a way of supporting her, and for a split second, she resents this, resents him for trying to sound like he's lost as much as she has. She resents him for maybe feeling more than she does—how dare he feel it when she can't, when she can only hear her grief as if from a great distance? She knows some animal part of her is feeling this grief, is keening with it, but she's split away from this animal part, even as she falls to her knees and crawls after her sister, even as they collapse against the futon mattress folded against the wall, and her sister says, "She killed herself." The older daughter had guessed a car crash with how their mom had been driving. She doesn't know how to process this news. The older daughter has become a camera, a cool, clear lens. She's become cool and clear as glass. She can record everything; she can't feel a thing.

"Oh, shit," Elizabeth says after we've been crying, stunned, for a time that feels like it could be hours, or a blink. "Dad. We were on the phone with Dad."

"What should we do?" I ask. Feeling has started to enter my limbs again. All my nerves are jangled. I seem to have forgotten how to breathe. Asher's baby swing goes back and forth, back and forth, its mechanical heart beat creaking through the room as he sleeps slumped in its seat.

"I don't want to tell him over the phone." Her eyes are sharp, determined. "I don't want him to be alone when he finds out. Let's say we're coming down to see him. We can tell him there."

This seems like the best thing to do. She calls and apologizes for taking so long to get back to him; she says the police had wanted more identifying information about Mom; she tries to set the stage to break the news later, when we're together.

I can hear him through the phone. "I can tell you're keeping something from me," he says. "What are you keeping from me?" Elizabeth's face crumples the way it did when the coroner's office called.

"She's dead!" she cries again. "She's dead!" and the starkness of the phrase hits me in the gut. "She died" would have sounded different—a process, a verb—like the "she" still had some agency, but "She's dead" wipes out the "she" completely. She's dead. She's gone. And it's the truth. It's the most honest way to say it.

Our mom is dead. She's dead, and I was the last person to talk to her, at least the last person in our family. I was the person who made her run away. The last word she ever said to me was *LIFE.*

I try to disappear into that white place again, that clear place, that empty place, but it's sealed itself off from me. I'm stuck here.

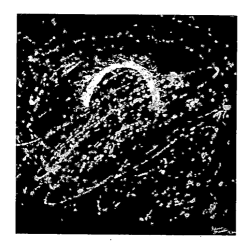

ROCHELLE'S RHAPSODY

[TEXT ON SCREEN: This painting is homage to my sister
Rochelle, whose lifelong battle with mental illness was
only correctly diagnosed a year before her death in 1999
as Hereditary Coproporphyria.]

ARLENE: This painting is about my sister, who had many
emotional and psychological problems. I painted it
to *Rhapsody in Blue* and of course, as you can see, I
was inspired by Pollack. I actually had the canvas on
the floor; I was blasting *Rhapsody in Blue*; I had my
paint in bottles—I had to find bottles that were for
hair dye that had nice little holes in them so I could
get small drips, and I was just kind of all over the
place, really dancing around the canvas to *Rhapsody
in Blue*.

Pollack is, of course, one of the early abstract expressionists, and he was quite well known for a couple of things. In the first place, he didn't have a center to his canvas, and so it was all visible from any side; there was no, no center at all, and I was really following that idea of his. Also, the abstract expressionists liked to express their inner emotions—they were putting all of the angst in their artwork, and I think I'm very much doing that with the history, the sad history, of my sister.

She had her first breakdown at the age of twenty-two. I was sixteen, and, uh, this, you know, I did put a center in. This is symbolic of electroshock therapy. She had, uh, you know, depression; she heard voices.

(TEXT ON SCREEN: Low sodium levels and the increase of the liver enzyme precursors, porphobiligens, can cause mental problems. All psychotic patients should be tested during an active episode.) [Note: ARLENE was never tested during a psychotic episode. ARLENE never believed she was having a psychotic episode.]

ARLENE: She had these auditory hallucinations that went on and on. She was never really diagnosed properly—maybe schizophrenic, but not really; maybe, um, manic depressive, but she really didn't fit that profile, either. But she was loaded up on all kinds of tranquilizers. She had this horrible electroshock therapy, things going on in the early '50s before they used to put you out for that, and toward the end of her life, when she was sixty-five, she still talked about electroshock therapy being the worst thing that

ever happened to her, transcending lung cancer and a
broken hip that left her in a wheelchair and all sorts
of horrible things. But she did recall that as being
the worst memory.

So, I lost my lack of center when I added the silver
crown that to me is symbolic of the electroshock
therapy.

Mom,

A few years ago, I contacted my old gastroenterologist by e-mail to see if I could get the medical records from when I was a teenager. It was weird to see Dr. Hanauer's picture online; he had aged, of course, but still had a boyishness about him—he was the "young one" in the practice, the pup compared to the venerable Dr. Kirschner. I was scared to see the records, scared to see the doctors' perceptions of me, their judgments of this sick girl who was probably faking her symptoms, of her family who was so swept up in the whole thing, but I knew it was important to read these records, to see the situation from outside my own skewed experience. Dr. Hanauer said he remembered me and my family and was glad to hear I was doing so well. He apologized and said there had been a fire several years ago. All of the old files had burned. There was no record of me in the hospital at all. I wasn't sure if I was more disappointed or relieved.

Around the same time, I got a call from a detective in Oklahoma.

"Is this Gayle Brandeis?" he asked.

I said yes.

"Your son is looking for you," he said. "The son you gave away in 1985."

All I could say was "What?!"

"Your name is on the birth certificate," he told me.

I was seventeen in 1985, still a few months away from losing my virginity, but the call played with my head in such a way that part of me wondered if maybe I had blocked the whole traumatic episode from my mind. I started to feel a bit loopy, unsure of reality, unsure of memory. But I told the detective no, it must have been another Gayle Brandeis, or someone using a false name. He thanked me for my time and hung up.

My body has no recollection of giving birth in 1985. I believe my body. My body remembers being sick, pretending to be sick. My body remembers my three pregnancies, the stretch and glow and quease, the twinges and burrito cravings. Let the records burn; the whole history is written in my flesh.

And the body can have a sick sense of humor. As adults, Elizabeth and I have—weirdly, karmically—switched symptoms.

She now has colitis; I puke my guts up every few months, preceded by pain worse than labor, still undiagnosed, that often sends me to the ER. A sort of medical Freaky Friday; a dramatic conclusion to our "That's my house" game.

Neither of us want to be sick at this point in our lives, but our bodies have another idea entirely—our bodies have found a way to have the last laugh.

Michael calls Matt to share the news about my mom's death and ask him to pick up Hannah at school, and we head out to my Honda to drive to Oceanside. I haven't been outside for a week. The air almost feels like a slap.

I am so grateful Elizabeth and Michael hadn't left before the call from the coroner's office came in. What would it have been like to get the news if I was home alone? Would I have fainted? Would my milk have dried up on the spot?

It takes us a while to figure out how to attach the base of Asher's car seat—all of us are fumble-handed, shaky—but we finally cinch the seatbelt through it, then click in the car seat, covered with owls, and strap Asher snugly inside. My mom gave me this car seat a few weeks ago, asking Michael to lug the box that contained it and the matching stroller all the way to the restaurant at the end of the Oceanside pier where we had our family baby shower the same weekend as Dad's ninetieth birthday party. It feels strange that she bought it for me and the first time we're using it is to deal with her death.

Elizabeth and I slip into the backseat on either side of Asher while Michael climbs into the front, our chauffeur. Asher falls asleep quickly on the road; we drape a gauzy receiving blanket over the car seat to keep the sun off his face, but I can't help but peer under it every few minutes to make sure he's breathing. Most of the time, my sister and I gaze at each other, our cheeks pressed against the nubby tan cloth of the seat. I feel like I could look into her eyes forever—the sun is turning them green, flecked with gold. She's the only person who knows exactly how I'm feeling right now, grief strung taut between us, her eyes keeping me rooted, keeping me present.

"Oh, Gayley," she says, and our eyes fill with tears. She pulls a packet of tissues from her bag and I notice that beneath where it says "Open," it says "Soulever" in French—soul ever—and it makes me wonder if it's a sign that means there's a soul, something that goes on forever, something I haven't ever really believed.

Open. Soul ever.

I want to believe it now. I want to be open to the possibility, but all I keep thinking is how my mom will never see all the familiar landmarks along this much traveled road again—she'll never see those terraced vineyards, that curved concrete bridge, the sign for the town named Rainbow. She'll never see anything.

We turn onto Highway 76, drive past the fruit stands where you can get twenty avocados for five dollars, past the flower stand where we bought an arrangement shaped like a turkey on our way to her house for Thanksgiving a year ago, not anticipating any of this—the wedding, the baby, her death—past the rolling hills covered with brown grass that looks like velvet, that looks like it would be soft if you were to roll down it, but would really be dry, prickly, would raise welts on my skin, past the fields of strawberries and horse ranches, the road curving gently, a road that often makes Michael car sick, but he is fine now, driving with purpose, driving his sleeping baby, driving two grieving women who don't know what to say, who keep looking into one another's eyes, then looking out the window at the trees, the shimmering yellow leaves.

When we arrive at my dad's duplex, we find him stoic, philosophical.

"I couldn't breathe when you told me," he says, "but then I sat outside and felt the sun on my face and started to feel better."

It's hard to believe he can be so calm, but we are grateful. He sets the tone for all of us. His apartment feels serene; it doesn't have the same nervous energy that had filled my house after the call. His complex is built along a ridge and when you look out the living room window, you can see across a valley. So much space; so many houses. People are just going about their normal lives in the world as our lives have entered this weird state of suspended animation. Maybe we're not the only ones. How many other people out there are mourning their own dead? How many roofs out there shelter someone's grief? How many neighbors belong to this same strange club we've just entered?

Elizabeth and I search the Yellow Pages for Oceanside funeral homes. There are some hassles involved with having our mom's body delivered over county lines, and we need to secure a funeral home to receive her. We make some calls, hear recordings along the lines of "Welcome to Happy Endings Funeral Home, a division of Respectful Memorial Corporation." Death as commodity. "Where is the funeral home from *Six Feet Under*?" Elizabeth asks and it feels good to have a brief laugh. We decide upon Oceanside Mortuary, which has been around since 1924, and Elizabeth makes the arrangements over the phone.

"I think we need to eat," my dad says as the sun starts to lower in the sky, and he's right; we had forgotten to eat lunch. Did we even eat breakfast? I can't remember. The day is a blur already. Michael leaves to pick up food from Chin's, where we had had a raucous family dinner over my dad's ninetieth birthday weekend last month—a long table full of siblings and cousins and hilarity. My mom had skipped that meal, claiming she was heading toward a diabetic coma; she had reclined on her couch like a dramatic Camille, the back of one hand draped on her forehead. Elizabeth and I had rolled our eyes when we left her house; it had been a relief to enter the dim restaurant, that room full of laughter.

I never expected my dad to outlive my mom. I've been afraid of his death all my life. He was so much older than my mom, so much older than all of my friends' dads; whenever he went out of town on business, I was scared he had died and my mom just wasn't sure how to break it to me. When he called at night, I imagined she had hired an impersonator. I didn't believe he was alive until he walked through the door again.

I can't stop wondering how my mom died. Elizabeth wanted to wait until we were all together to give us the details and she hasn't been ready yet. Pills seem most obvious. Maybe in a different fancy hotel wearing one of her fancy nightgowns, opera playing in the background, a soprano ushering her into oblivion.

Michael returns with the food and we sit around my dad's dining table, chewing softly. We stare at the take out cartons of brown rice and bean curd in brown sauce; we stare at the cartons of cashew chicken and shrimp and pea pods; we stare at the smears of sauce on our places, the rice collapsing under the weight of Chinese vegetables—giant slabs of black mushroom, ears of baby corn. Sometimes one of us cries a little bit; sometimes another one does.

We didn't think we'd have an appetite, but we do.

"This feels like sustenance," my sister says, breaking the silence, and it does; the food feels good, elementally good, like it's feeding some place deep inside us.

Still, my dad has trouble finding his mouth with his fork; he opens his mouth like a baby waiting to be fed and the fork misses, jabbing his cheek, sending rice onto his lap. He looks older than I can remember seeing him. I am tempted to take his fork from his hand, feed him myself.

Elizabeth breaks the silence again.

"She hanged herself," she says softly, and I can't take this in, not fully. "Hanged herself" sounds funny to me, wrong; shouldn't it be "hung"? She "hung herself"? Who decided that "hanged" was better than "hung"? If I use "hung" out loud will it sound ignorant, like I don't know the proper terminology for my mother's death?

"Where?" Michael asks.

"A parking garage in Pasadena," she says. Pasadena, just like Michael had imagined. It happened around 4:50 yesterday afternoon, just when I was ushering Michael's sister and nephews out the door. A worker found her this morning.

The wordplay in my head—*hanged, hung, hanged, hung*—keeps the feelings at bay for a moment, but now they start to rise in my throat, along with a clump of soy-soaked rice. Hanging is so much more brutal, more violent, than anything I could have imagined. I swallow hard, keenly aware of my own neck, the breath moving inside.

ARLENE: Well, Rochelle, at the age of sixty-four, when
she was having surgery, and after my daughter was
diagnosed with porphyria, I asked her doctor to test
[Rochelle] for porphyria and, sure enough, she had a
positive for hereditary corproporphyria. Well, I was
told that's the rarest of the rare porphyrias, and I
can't help but wonder if there are a lot of people in
psychiatric wards who have breakdowns and then they're
fine, they don't respond to traditional treatment; I
can't help but think that this is more common than we
know, and I think any time they have a psychiatric
patient, particularly if they also have abdominal
pain, if there's also regurgitation, if there's also
some kind of skin rash, these should be red flags to
test for porphyria. How different her life would
have been if we had a correct diagnosis. All of the
worst medications that can be given to someone with
porphyria—she was given barbiturates, tranquilizers,
lithium, all of which made her very nauseated—they
exacerbated the condition; it really needs to be
looked at.

I'm sure there are, I mean, there are a million people
who are being treated for mental problems. She's not
the only one. She's not the only one who has this,
and it's my understanding that my father had a sister
who was dead long before I was born who had the
same problem that she did. And, um, so it's a real
important message, and psychiatrists really have to
read up on this, do the twenty-minute test.

Every time she went on a diet, she seemed to have one of these psychotic episodes (crying), and carbohydrates are such an important treatment in porphyria (wipes away tears). It's really so simple and so dramatically important.

Mom,

Your delusional episodes and my vomiting episodes were pretty similar in that I was never prepared for either. They took me by surprise every time. They shouldn't have; they happened on a regular basis—sometimes months would go by, sometimes even a full year—but they kept coming back and I kept getting caught off guard. Neither of us had been diagnosed, so there were no labels to anchor us.

Here are some things, over the course of nineteen years, doctors thought might be causing my vomiting episodes:

- Porphyria
- Abdominal migraines
- Cyclical vomiting syndrome
- Pseudo-obstructive motility disorder

Here are some things, over the course of sixteen years, the family thought might be causing your delusional episodes:

- Porphyria
- Schizophrenia
- Borderline personality disorder
- Mismanaged diabetes
- A lesion on your brain

Between episodes, I would let myself get lulled into a false sense that everything was okay, that I was healthy, that you were sane, and then—*BLAM!*—back into the muck.

NOVEMBER 30–DECEMBER 1, 2009

Elizabeth decides to sleep at our dad's place to keep him company. I want to stay, too, but we didn't bring enough diapers or clothes or toiletries for an extended stay. When Michael and Asher and I are halfway home, Father Paschal calls and serenades me with a heavily accented rendition of Michael Jackson's "You Are Not Alone." Michael Jackson died earlier this year, too. He and my mom were both utterly alone at the end. I press my forehead to the backseat window and watch the dark world stream by.

Elizabeth calls the next day and suggests I get in touch with my midwife to ask about remedies I might take to help keep my milk production up in the midst of mourning. Karen recommends agrimony and Rescue Remedy for shock, aconite and ignatia for grief. Our friends Jenn and Nancy pick up the tinctures and homeopathic pellets, along with white chestnut to help stanch unwanted thoughts and a pear tree we can plant with the placenta when the time is right. Nancy drapes a shawl embossed with a picture of Kwan Yin, the Bodhisattva of compassion, around my shoulders as I cry and cry and cry against her chest. Jenn holds Asher, looks at his wise, direct, gaze, and says, "He was brought here to be a healer." I don't want him to feel he has to be his mother's healer his whole life, but for now, I'll take it.

My mom's body has been delivered to Oceanside Mortuary. My dad and Elizabeth go to view her. They stand in the doorway, peek into the room the way you would if someone was sleeping. They had been told she had marks on her face—the "marbling" that happens with a hanging—and don't want to get too close.

The word "marbling" makes me think of my mom's dad; he was a butcher who killed chickens in the back of his little market

on State Street in Chicago. My mom watched him hold their feath-
ery bodies and slit their throats, bright blood gushing to the floor.
He didn't kill cows, but she had been taken to the stockyards on
a field trip, her class piled into buses and led single file into the
slaughter house, the cows shuffling and mooing single file, too,
until the blade came down and their heads clunked to the floor.
They weren't cows anymore—just bodies, just meat, ready to skin
and send to her father's market, ready to be cut into steaks, ground
into hamburger, their rumps carried in a cardboard box on her father's shoulder on the train so her mother could roast them and
bring them to the table each Sunday; bodies that hung in her father's cold-storage room, their glistening fat streaked with blue,
marbling their flesh.

It feels funny to not be at the mortuary with my dad and sister, but
it feels good to be home. My breasts keep having chills through
them, like I have a fever, but only in that part of my body. My body
wants to be still, to sit with my baby in my arms and shiver and
be still.

When Elizabeth calls after they get back to our dad's place, she
tells me our mom looked peaceful, a blanket pulled up to her chin.
She says it was a relief to see how peaceful she looked, a relief to
confirm it was her. Neither she or our dad had truly believed it until
they saw her in person.

I am on the phone much of the day.

Friends and colleagues call to congratulate me on the baby,
and I find myself blurting out "My mom hanged herself!" or "My
mom killed herself!," shocking them into speechlessness. I have
no filter. I feel as if I have no skin. I am a flayed creature, one raw,
exposed nerve.

My first husband, Matt, calls. He says—he urges—that none
of us should feel guilty or feel there was something else we could
have done. "Her modus operandi was making people feel guilty,"

he says. "That should die with her." I am flooded with gratitude. He knows me more than I had given him credit for. Of course he does. We had once loved one another madly.

His mom, Patricia, calls a bit later. "I don't know how to comfort you," she says, "but I hope you can find some peace in the fact that she's found peace."

Michael's mother hasn't said a word to me yet, hasn't acknowledged my mom's death. She won't for many weeks, even though we'll see her several times.

Every time the phone rings the rest of the day, Michael answers first so I'll have a chance to collect myself before I speak.

After night falls and the calls die down, Michael turns on *So You Think You Can Dance*, one of our favorite TV shows, so we can distract ourselves, numb ourselves out. In one duet, a woman dances a smooth waltz with a long, flowing blue scarf around her neck. I think of all the scarves my mom wore—short ones that looked like tourniquets; long ones that draped down over her arty Chico's outfits. She never went out without a scarf, self-conscious about her aging neck. The only time her neck was bare in public was when she went swimming. Before she took to wearing scarves, she would often cut her neck out of photos of our visits together before she sent them to me. Sometimes she'd cut out her whole body; she'd just be a head floating next to us on the print.

I start to weep, to hyperventilate. Michael wraps his arms around me. The dance music surges through the air like a dramatic soundtrack, accompanied by the heartbeat creak of Asher's baby swing.

"Do you think she did it with a scarf?" I ask him.

"I was wondering the same thing," he says.

I watch the dancer on TV, scarf floating behind her like a wing, and picture my mom wrapping a scarf around her neck for a final, fatal time.

DR. NEVILLE PIMSTONE, gastroenterologist: And a third attack symptom which can occur is disordered brain function, which can lead to a form which has been known as the madness of King George, possibly Vincent van Gogh.

DESIREE LYON HOWE, founder/executive director, American Porphyria Foundation: Historians feel that madness of King George due to porphyria—and I'll digress a minute; the reason that they feel that King George had porphyria is because of this sort of purpley red urine, which can happen with someone who has a porphyria attack, because he had these periods of mania that would come and go. . . . His royal physicians were supposed to put down everything in a report about the quote unquote "royal body," which they did, and many years later, as these were being investigated, uh, and as many other family members were discovered to have had the disease, historians put two and two together and feel that he had porphyria. Now, how that has affected and impacted our own country is that during the Revolutionary War, King George would have these attacks intermittently and Parliament would try very hard to get him to concentrate and increase the troops and increase the monies for these colonists, but he would listen and then go into another attack and he would not allow them to move forward, or he would be sick at the time, and one of the things that he has actually said was that the great and mighty British Empire could not possibly be beaten by this group of ill-trained militia, and really, that was probably true, but since they couldn't get him to be well long enough, it greatly impacted what happened to our country.

Mom,

November 6, 1994, was a real turning point for our family.

When Dad called that day, I could tell something was wrong. His "Hi, honey," had a strange, flat weight to it. Before I could ask what was up, he said, "Mom attacked me." You had been attacking him verbally, emotionally, for a year, but his voice told me this was different.

"What happened?" I asked, every muscle braced. Hannah scooted across the front of the burgundy velour couch. I was so tightly wound; if she had tumbled, I could have flown across the room and caught her mid-fall.

He took a breath and said, "I was standing at the sink and I felt something warm on the back of my neck and gefilte fish rose up my throat."

None of this made any sense. I could picture him standing at the sink at the house on Hibbard Road in Winnetka, looking out into the neighbor's back yard that butted up against theirs, the one filled with gaudy animal statuary. I could picture him rinsing ge-filte fish brine off a plate. The rest was a mystery.

"It was a stun gun," he said. "She thought it would give me a heart attack."

"Oh, Papa." I could barely see straight. You tried to kill him. You actually tried to kill him. I scooped Hannah up and held her close, my heart thudding against her back. "You have to get out of there. You have to get out of there!"

"I have," he said. "I'm at the Marriott by the airport."

"Good, good," I said, relieved but shaky. "Did you press charges?"

Maybe you were in custody. Maybe this was the chance we'd been looking for, the chance to finally get you some help. I took in a deep whiff of Hannah's hair as she squirmed in my arms; the scent of sunlight and dirt and shampoo calmed me. She wrestled herself away and went crawling across the room.

"I couldn't," he said, his voice breaking down. "I couldn't do that to her."

You called a little while later. I wanted to scream at you, but, as usual, the words froze in my throat. I told myself it was because I didn't want to scare Hannah by raising my voice. I was grateful Arin was in preschool so I wouldn't have to answer any questions about the call.

"Your father attacked me," you said, and the room started to spin.

"What?" I asked. "What happened?" I knew I shouldn't believe you, but part of me felt off balance, my mind taking in the remote possibility that Dad could have been the aggressor. I hated when I let that happen, when I let your delusions infect me.

"He hit me on the head with some black thing," you said, and just as quickly, my world shifted back to its original axis.

Every creative writing book I'd ever read drilled in the importance of specific detail. I knew right away that Dad's story—the warmth on his neck, the gefilte fish in his throat—was more accurate and authentic than "some black thing."

"If he did, it was self-defense," I said, emboldened. Hannah looked over at me and giggled. "He said you attacked him with a stun gun."

"I did no such thing," you said, your voice getting higher. "And I have the hospital report to prove it."

I learned later from Dad that after the stun gun failed, you went to the garage and smacked the door of your Thunderbird repeatedly against your head until you raised a bruise, then went to the Highland Park Hospital emergency room to report your husband had beaten you. I found the paperwork after your death. The doctor had sketched out a head with a smiley face—it looked like a jack-o'-lantern or snowman, something jaunty and festive with round eyes, a triangle nose and an upturned grin. A little area around the left temple is scribbled in with black ink, "2 1/2 x 3 1/2 cm hematoma" scrawled next to it; on the drawing, it looks less like an injury than a decoration, a flower on a Day of the Dead skull. The report reads "Ambulates into ER for c/o being hit by heavy black object on L side of head by husband, + bump, felt dizzy, now improved, no LOC or HA. PERL. Vision felt blurred, now improved. In process of divorce, no prior hx of physical abuse by husband, pt refuses social service at this time, number given to pt for referral in future if needed. Pt. at Police Station in Winnetka, pt refusing to make report." You were given a cold pack to press to your head and were reportedly "in good spirits" two hours later.

While I wished Dad had pressed charges, I was grateful you had not, grateful some part of you knew you shouldn't send your husband to jail for something he didn't do.

Dad never moved back into the house. You didn't speak to each other for the next three years.

DECEMBER 2, 2009

Michael and Asher and I drive back out to my dad's house so we can be with him and Elizabeth and figure out our next step. Elizabeth and I have decided any memorial is going to be just family. Our siblings from our dad's first marriage are flying in—our brother Jon and his wife, Magdalene, from New York, our sister Sue and her husband, Larry, from Maryland. Our cousin Bobby is flying in from Washington State. Matt will drive Arin and Hannah out from Riverside. The only nonfamily members invited will be Nancy and Jenn, who are like family, who have been instrumental during so many transitions in my life. Still, we want to let people in my mom's small circle know about her death. Michael calls her friend Richard. "Life is shit," Richard says and hangs up the phone. The few women Elizabeth calls who had once been my mom's friends are sure our dad is somehow responsible for her death; Elizabeth has to tell them that she was delusional, that all her accusations were false. One woman asks, "Are you sure?" and I watch Elizabeth close her eyes as she says, "Yes. Yes, I'm sure." Our mom's spiritual teacher, she of the "what your car says about you" fame, says some platitudes about death and shows no sign of sympathy.

I message a cousin—my mom's sister's son—via Facebook; he passes the news along to his mom, who e-mails me. "I'm shocked and deeply saddened by this horrible event," Sylvia writes. "I suppose the fact that your mom and I never resolved our ongoing problems makes it even worse." I still don't know what all the ongoing problems were between them, but I'm grateful to be connected with her again.

Father Paschal calls and tells me more about my mom's last day. His accent makes his words tricky to understand, but I gather a few things:

- She went to three masses. At the first one, she had approached him and handed him the letter she ultimately left for us. The letter asking for more time.
- She spent the whole day in La Placita, staying in his office between masses. He gave her a Bible to read, and a book on depression. She told him she wasn't depressed. He says she seemed happy; she seemed like she was with God (but still, he took her car keys, knowing she shouldn't drive).
- They had a meal together; she fell in love with a little girl and shared an apple with her.
- She called him her son; he called her "Mom." His own mom died six or seven years ago. "You have an African brother," he says.
- She gave the church a thousand dollars in cash. Maybe this was the money Duke Bristow had told me about.

"We all die," says Father Paschal. "We just never know the time. This was her time. It's not up for us to question God's choice." He says we should know we did all we could.

I thank him for helping my mom on her final day, for helping all of us. It feels weird that she gave the church so much money—part of me wonders if she was pressured into it—but it also warms my heart. It's good to know one of her final acts was a generous one.

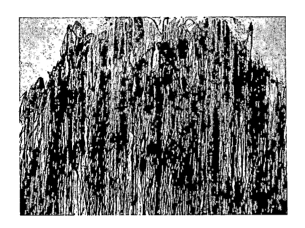

PATERNAL DNA

ARLENE: This painting is called *Paternal DNA*. Of course,
it's about my father. The porphyria side of the family
I believe comes from my father only because I know he
had a sister who died quite young and long before I
was born, and it sounded like she had the same problem
my sister, Rochelle, had, and, um, this rare form of
hereditary corpora porphyria. My father had a very
difficult end in life; he had two amputations, um,
strokes. These corners kind of reminded me of those
amputations for some reason; I made a connection to
them that I feel. The drip painting is maybe in the
style of Morris Louis; he talked about controlled
drip painting. I, um, didn't think about it until
the art piece was finished because I wasn't familiar
with Morris Louis at the time I did the painting, but
he's in just about every contemporary art museum and
does a lot of this type of thing, only fewer drips
and a lot of raw canvas. The music I used was *Spanish*

Rhapsody, and his family originally came from Spain, from south central Spain, and there's a city in south central Spain called Bailen, which is my maiden name (Baylen), and there was a castle of Bailen, which is now (word unclear), which is owned by the government, and I always jokingly say that I want to go back and claim my room at the castle. . . . The family left during the Spanish Inquisition, went to England and then to Russia when there were a couple of Russian czarinas who were the daughters of British dukes and duchesses, so how the family got from Spain to England to Russia is really interesting, and I'm trying to do a genealogy search, but his end was very difficult and I know the porphyria came from his side of the family.

My father got sick when I was a teenager; I was fifteen. Diabetes is another thing in the family that I understand is very connected to Ehlers-Danlos syndrome, and many people I speak to who have porphyria are also diabetic, so I've been diabetic for about fifteen years and it's a real juggling act to try to eat enough carbohydrates to stay healthy and to also manage a blood sugar thing. So I swim; I swim every other day; I'm on the treadmill, and that's the way I manage to keep myself healthy with it, but my father's illness was really so dreadful. It began when I was fifteen—he died when I was twenty—so for those five years, he was bedridden, he had strokes, he had these amputations, and my mother cared for him.

Mom,

Your divorce took a long time.

You went through several lawyers, dropping one after the other when they couldn't find the hidden assets you were so adamant existed.

You went on a quest to find these assets yourself. You sent subpoenas to everyone associated with Dad's business, and to people you imagined were associated with Dad in some sinister way. You drove to a company in Cuyahoga Falls, Ohio, you thought Dad was funneling money through, a company you said the Ohio Secretary of State didn't recognize. You wrote, "When I drove by, three people were in the window trying to figure out who I was. I didn't go inside. They must have called [name redacted] to confirm the name I used, Kimberly Bateman." You were always reinventing yourself, taking on new names for new tasks. As a child, you gave yourself the middle name you kept for the rest of your life, June.

You left behind boxes and briefcases full of divorce documents, boxes and briefcases full of petitions for dissolution of marriage and property settlement agreements and memoranda of understanding and angry letters you wrote to your lawyers and letters back from your lawyers saying they could not help you the way that you wanted.

You kept trying. You knew the money was out there. You were sure you would find the right person to help you find the motherlode.

DECEMBER 2009

The line between dream and reality starts to blur.

One night, I wake Michael at 3 a.m. and tell him, "My nipples are cracked, my breasts are full and they're on speaker phone." I tell him the contestants have gone seven rounds already, and Asher hasn't had his turn. When Asher nurses, I imagine he's on *Top Chef,* creating an amazing dish. I know I'm not making sense, but somehow it is all clear in my head. Another night, I tell Michael that my mom had so much love in her car trunk and now I'm channeling it through my breasts. I wonder if this was how my mom felt, trying to assure us her delusions were real. I am comforted by the fact that I can laugh about my strange visions; she never could.

She keeps entering my dreams:

- I am in an airport, walking toward a departure gate. My mom is walking in the other direction, on the other side of a rope. Her face has no expression. She walks right past without acknowledging me at all.
- I am in a theater, possibly for a dress rehearsal of a show. My mom walks up to me, angry, and suddenly we are on the steps of the house in Winnetka, the house I so hated. My mom shoves me down, hard—I can feel this in a visceral way—and lunges toward my neck like a vampire. I wake gasping and shouting, dizzy with adrenaline.
- I am in our house, although it is not really our house—bigger, more modern. Some of my students are renovating it for us. Suddenly, without any warning, my mother and I shoot up into the air, disoriented, the floor gone, everything askew; I realize that this is some sort of natural disaster, an earthquake, maybe. I yell "Mama!" and cling to her before we start to fall.

And then it seems my mom comes to visit me for real. I am lying on my right side, nursing Asher, when someone lays a hand on my shoulder. Michael is in the kitchen; my sister is with our dad. No one else is in the house; certainly no one else is in the bedroom. The hand presses down, firm, but loving. My whole body stiffens. I don't believe in ghosts, but I'm convinced it's her. I'm not ready for her comfort, her apology. I lift my shoulder to my ear to shrug off the touch. The pressure leaves and I immediately feel awful; I want it, want her, back.

When I was a little girl, I would prepare myself for the possibility of a ghost or alien visit. "They're part of the world, just like us," I would tell myself as I hunkered under my Holly Hobby comforter. I would remind myself to stay calm, to not be afraid, to listen to whatever the ghost or alien had to tell me.

All that preparation, and I still can't handle her ghost.

DESIREE LYON HOWE: So, as an outcome of my own suffering, not just physical suffering but emotional suffering that no one believed me, no one believed I was as ill as I was, I decided that other people needed to meet one another and learn everything we could learn. So, starting with another gentleman whose wife had the same problem, we began the foundation twenty-seven years ago at my kitchen table, and it grew and grew and grew as patients reached out to try to find one another and to learn what they could, and also physicians.

Mom,

You became a crusader for divorce reform, renaming yourself A. J. Brand—A. J. for Arlene June; Brand shaved off from
Brandeis, itself a fairly recent graft onto the family tree. At the
urging of his brother-in-law, Dad had changed his last name from
Bransky to Brandeis during the McCarthy era, when having a
Russian name was bad for business. He chose Brandeis because
he deeply admired Louis Brandeis, plus it let him keep the first
few letters of his family name, let his name continue to assert his
Jewishness.

You chose a pseudonym for safety, you said—you were sure if
you used your real name for your divorce reform work, Dad's goons
would track you down. Still, you gave a little nod to your married
name at the end of one of your mission statements, writing:

> As Supreme Court Justice Louis Brandeis has said, "Sunlight is
> the best cure for bacteria." The more sunlight generated in the
> form of publicity, education and empowerment, the sooner the
> "bacteria" in a portion of the "divorce system" can be eliminated.

You created the National Foundation for Financially Abused
Women—NOFAW. This always sounded like a donkey braying the
words "No fault" to me, *NO FAAAAAAWWW,* which felt fitting;
you never thought anything was your fault. You convinced a local
reporter to attend a meeting you held in your living room; he published an article about it in the *Winnetka Talk*—"Men Get the Gold,
Women Get the Shaft"—and soon you were flooded with letters
from women experiencing true financial abuse. Soon you had a
real organization on your hands.

The *Chicago Tribune* took note; Eric Zorn wrote an article published July 23, 1995, that read, in part:

[W]omen call or write with such stories so consistently that I have come to believe the rough outlines: concealed assets, secret sources of income, false bankruptcies, looted insurance policies, illicit stock transfers—in other words, men playing for keeps, working the system to maximize their gains in divorce and to leave their wives with as little as possible.

A Winnetka woman who goes by the nom de guerre A. J. Brand has labeled such shenanigans "financial abuse," a problem that attracts far less attention and public response than the spousal violence of what we call domestic abuse, but one that Brand believes is just as common and devastating.

Brand, 56, who is separated from a husband of 28 years whom she accuses of dreadful domestic piracy, began meeting earlier this year with four other middle-age, upper-middle-income women in similar circumstances. They had splintered off a conventional divorce-oriented support group, where the focus was on custody issues that no longer concerned them.

The informal gatherings at which they swapped stories and strategies caught the attention of *Pioneer Press* columnist Alan Henry. His write-up inspired several dozen North Shore women who felt they had been victimized in the same way to contact Brand, who in turn incorporated the not-for-profit National Organization for Financially Abused Women.

Officials at the National Organization for Women and the Older Women's League in Washington said they knew of no other support organization in the country with such a focus, even though the financial burden of divorce still most commonly falls on women. One often-cited study says the average woman with children experiences a 73 percent decline in standard of living after a divorce, while her ex-husband experiences a 43 percent increase. A Social Security Administration study of recipients shows that one in four elderly divorced women live below the poverty line, compared to just one in 20 elderly married women.

NOFAW, which now claims 140 members, is working to help women going through marital strife, separation and divorce become economically savvy by linking them with accountants, investigators, financial planners and mediators who are hip to husband tricks. Brand is at NOW's annual convention in Cincinnati this weekend soliciting both new members and specialists for a planned self-help directory. She said NOFAW is also pushing for reforms in tax and pension laws and attorney codes of conduct.

The ironic thing is that Dad paid all your bills and sent you half his income every month. The man who was supposedly abusing you financially funded the founding of NOFAW.

DECEMBER 4, 2009

Jon and Sue and their spouses arrive and we hug and talk and cry and talk and it feels so good, this talking, so free. It was impossible to have deep, honest conversations when my mom was around. Jon and Magdalene tell us how hard it was for them to even visit Dad. "It would always hurt him," Magdalene says in tears; after their visits, my mom would ramp up her accusations about Jon and our dad being in cahoots, about them plotting against her. She couldn't just let our dad enjoy a visit with his son; there was always a cost.

There is a sweetness to all this talking, all this grieving. Elizabeth tells us how easily she's slipped into a retiree's schedule—early dinner, early bedtime—how sweet it's been to stay with Dad, to speak with him so openly. We're all grateful to have a patriarch who—for all the silences in our family—is encouraging us to be honest now.

"Can you imagine what it would have been like if Dad had died first?" I ask Elizabeth and her eyes widen at the thought. Our mom would have gone on and on about trying to find his hidden fortune; she would have gone on and on about his supposed deviousness. It would have added another painful layer to the loss. Now we can face grief head on—at least as head on as we can with all the questions surrounding her death.

Our dad arranges for a rabbi to swing by, and when she arrives in her purple and blue knit yarmulke and attempts to facilitate conversation between us, we realize we've already done this, ourselves; we've already gone deep together. What helps most is her leading us through the Kaddish, the Hebrew mourner's prayer. We read the transliteration from the yellow photocopies she brought with her, and it is comforting to know that millions upon millions of people have read the same words in the midst of loss.

"Why don't we go around the circle and say what you'll each miss about Arlene," the rabbi suggests, prayer still thick in the air. Sue says, "She was my stepmom and I loved her." Larry says she made him laugh. Jon talks about how his anger toward our mom has turned to compassion. Magdalene calls her ballsy, a spitfire. Elizabeth says how much she appreciates the parenting advice Mom gave her—answer every question your child asks; she appreciates how our mom taught us to question, to seek justice. Dad says, "I fell in love with her the moment I saw her and I never stopped loving her." Michael says she came to represent family. I talk about how she thought outside the box, how she taught her girls to think outside the box; I talk about how she used words to make the world a better place. "I remember her soft skin," I find myself saying. "Her hands."

I stop there. The rabbi asks if I've said everything I want to and I nod, even though there's so much I could say about my mom, so much more I could say about her graceful, elegant, hands. She had been a hand model when she was a young woman; there are close-up photos of her hands facing one another, gently curved in supplication. They remind me of tulips; they remind me of wings.

I look down at my own hands—they look so much like my mom's now, her older hands, wormy veins rising on top. My hands aren't as soft as hers were, though—the skin on my fingertips is papery, peeling. This started when I left Matt—I thought I was having an allergic reaction to all the cardboard boxes during the move, but the peeling's continued off and on ever since. My dermatologist thinks I might be allergic to something—most likely my keyboard. My mom would never let this peeling happen to her hands; she would have been more proactive about treating them. I've tried various creams to no avail—she would have found one that worked. She would never pursue treatment for her mental illness, but her hands, she would treat. Her hands were always supple, graceful, except for the one pinky finger that rebelled, kinked itself into a jagged lightning bolt. It was her hands that did the work in the end, her hands that lifted the scarf or rope or whatever she used to make the noose, wrapped it around her neck. Her beautiful hands that—perhaps at this very moment—are being burned down to nothing but ash.

RE: SEARCH IV

Death by Hanging

The day before my novel *Delta Girls* came out, in 2010, I bought a large French educational poster titled "La Multiplication Vegetative," with drawings that detail several growing processes—"Les Metamorphoses Florales," featuring the growth cycle of a rose, "La Greffe," showing how to graph one tree to another, and "La Taille des Arbres Fruitiers," illustrating how a pear tree bears fruit. *Delta Girls* is set on a pear farm, and I thought the pears were a good omen; plus, I knew it would be nice to have a reminder of organic process in my writing space.

When my sister saw the poster the first time, she pointed to the word "ligature," where a cord binds a graft to a branch.

"That's the technical term used in a hanging," she told me. My sister had found some obscure hanging trivia since our mom's suicide—because of her, I knew that asparagus grows well beneath gallows, fed by the semen let loose by the hanged, and that weeping willows, our mom's favorite tree, are associated with that kind of death. She flinched, her face full of apology. "I hope I haven't ruined the picture for you."

She didn't ruin it, but she definitely changed my relationship with the poster. Now when I look at it, I am reminded by that word, that image, to look my mom's story straight in the face. The reality is always there; I don't want to shy away from it.

It took some time, but I finally started to do some of my own research on hanging.

I learned that hanging is the most common form of suicide worldwide, accounting for 53 percent of men and 39 percent of women who take their lives (in America, it's the second most common method behind gunshot for men, the second most common method behind poisoning for women).

I had assumed that the cause of death for those who hanged themselves was a broken neck, but learned the neck usually only breaks when someone is hanged from a gallows, known as a "drop" hanging. Most suicides by hanging are considered "suspension" hangings; the cause of death in these cases is compression of either the carotid artery (5kg of pressure required), the jugular vein (2kg of pressure), or the airway (15kg). Drop hangings are supposed to be less painful and faster than suspension hangings; I can barely stand to think about that, to think of any pain my mom might have felt, to think of how it might have taken a while for her to lose consciousness.

Hanging survivors report having seen flashing lights, having heard ringing sounds. I hope a real light show ushered my mom out of her life. Like being on a dance floor. Like going into hyperspace.

A couple of months before my mom's death, Lady Gaga pretended to hang herself on stage during the MTV Video Music Awards. I remember cries of protest by suicide survivor organizations, saying members had been traumatized by the image; I remember thinking—cruelly, I realize now—that these people were being overly sensitive. Now I understand completely.

Words related to suicide became serious triggers for me. I found myself going through elaborate verbal gymnastics to avoid using the word "hang," even in the most mundane and innocent of contexts. I'd say, "I want to . . . put that picture on the wall," or, "Could you . . . drape that towel on the hook for me, please?" For a while, I avoided playing "Words With Friends" on my phone because the pop-up ads for "Hanging With Friends" would jab me in the heart.

Glib references to hanging abound, as Elizabeth and I quickly discovered. "This yeast infection makes me want to kill myself" one of her colleagues said before she mimed wrapping a noose around her throat and letting her head drop to the side. An innocent offer of a game of hangman made me lose my breath.

"We can't expect the world to tiptoe on eggshells around us," Elizabeth and I would remind each other. We told each other that every time we had to confront an upsetting word or image, it helped us learn to cope. And at some point, I tricked myself into believing I was coping just fine. I pushed my pain beneath the surface, where it grew grotesque in silence and darkness, like a potato sprouting eyes.

MOM DIED BEFORE MY WEDDING

ARLENE: It's probably the one event in my life that of
all the sadnesses is really the saddest one for me.
Um, I painted to Dvorak's "Songs My Mother Taught
Me." Um, we were very connected (starts crying). She
was a great mom. Well, my mother died on January 13,
1967, which was just about five weeks before my wedding
and couldn't have been a more terrible time to deal
with her death, but, um, as you see, I was married
February 22, 1967, so it was a terrible time and still
a very painful memory.

Mom,

You had black-and-white promotional pictures taken as A. J. Brand, wearing glasses you thought made you look professorial, an uncomfortable smile on your face. You found a vocal coach to help give your speaking voice more authority, although whenever you attempted the lower register you had been trained to use, you sounded like you were trying to mimic a male cartoon character of some sort—Marvin the Martian, perhaps. You sent letters to every talk show you could find, from *Regis and Kathie Lee* to *Gadget Talk*. You appeared on a few shows produced in Chicago, both TV and radio. You started to gain more and more members. You created two sister organizations, the Coalition to End Financial Abuse in Marriage and the Coalition for Financial Fairness. You self-published a book, *A Guide to Divorce: Answers to Questions You Didn't Know to Ask*, although we were sure you had plagiarized it or had it ghost-written; the writing didn't sound like your own. You trademarked the terms "consumer of divorce" and "Divorce Empowerment." You organized a national conference, where you presented an award named for Olivia Goldsmith, author of *The First Wives' Club*, to Lorna Wendt, who had fought for half of her husband's General Electric fortune during their divorce. You had a plaque engraved to Wendt "In appreciation of your efforts to enhance and elevate the role of the homemaker in marriage." You did everything you could to enhance and elevate your own role as A. J. Brand. You did everything you could until the paranoia returned and you felt people were trying to undermine you, to wrest your divorce reform empire away from you, and you dissolved it all, yourself.

A few months before you died, you sent me this e-mail:

Subject: divorce reform

From: Arlene Brandeis arlenebrandeis@cox.net

To: me

In the event anyone cares about the correct detail:

The divorce reform I initiated is and was a state issue. I lobbied Illinois State Senator Kathy Parker in 1995 about "financial fairness in and during the divorce process." Many women after decades of marriage, often to professional, high income spouses ended with nothing and sometimes homeless.

It was during this process US Senator Carol Mosley Braun asked me to participate in a Pension Reform Committee.

Pension law (at my suggestion) was changed to require a spouse be notified if they opt for a larger pension payment during their lifetime.

That option leaves the surviving spouse with no pension income. That nasty surprise is why your sitter Ruby Cox (and thousands of women like her) was forced to baby sit or live in poverty after her (the spouse dies,) husband died.

I've been meaning to clarify that for a long time. Maybe you'll use it for my obituary some day.

It took me years to appreciate what you had done with NOFAW and its sister organizations. I was too mad at you for what you were doing to Dad, too unsure about how to talk to you, how to deal with your mix of delusion and activism. For years, I shrugged off that whole period of your life, dismissed it as part of your mental illness, didn't let myself see how much you had really accomplished. We didn't even mention NOFAW in your obituary, not specifically, although we did reference you had worked for social justice. The whole NOFAW chapter felt like a sad, ironic joke. Then last year, I got a Facebook message from a woman you had helped. You had been a true inspiration to her during her divorce, she wrote; you talked to her many times over the phone; you gave her the information she needed to protect herself; you gave her the motivation to move to another state with her children, to start law school at forty-three. "That my children and I could survive was in part attributable to your mom," she wrote. "I am thankful for that." I am thankful for that now, too.

All the out of town relatives are staying at a hotel near our dad's place. We gather there before we head to the Oceanside harbor for our mom's memorial. Cousin Bobby has made it from the airport. Matt has dropped off Arin and Hannah—it is so good to see them, to hug them, to just be with them. My beautiful kids. Nancy and Jenn arrive, too, bringing their warm, grounded energy.

We walk down the hallway. Just ahead of me, Elizabeth has birth and death in her hands—in her right, Asher, ensconced in his car seat; in her left, our mom's ashes in the silver bag from Oceanside Mortuary. The bag looks like something from a high end department store, Nordstrom's maybe, the paper thick and gleaming, letters elegant and white. Our mom would approve; she always aspired to luxury—it makes sense she would even after death. Only the best for her chips of bone.

Asher. Ashes.

The patterned jewel tone carpet makes light shoot dizzy inside my eyes. Elizabeth looks like the incarnation of Lady Justice as she walks ahead of me, or Lady Libra, birth and death balanced evenly on her scales. Asher/Ashes. Ashes/Asher. She stands tall, arms strong as she walks forward, bearing their equal weight.

I don't feel nearly as graceful, myself. I am stumbling down the hall, holding a diaper bag, a purse, the flimsy necessities, straps digging into my shoulders. I am leaking milk and blood; I am leaking and stumbling while my sister holds her head high between life's outermost poles, a steady pole herself, a fulcrum between two worlds.

Asher. . . . Ashes.

The owls on Asher's car seat are turquoise and orange and brown; his baby contraptions are way cuter than any available when my grown kids were little. It suddenly strikes me as funny that baby things are designed to be cute. I've come to realize over the past couple of days that newborns are terrifying. Asher is sweet and beautiful and fresh as a flower, but he is also terrifying. A wild animal. All hunger. No reason. We try to soften it up with owls, but there it is—the dark and glittering abyss in his tiny open mouth.

Asher, Ashes.

Just one letter apart. R and S, letters that sit next to each other in the alphabet, even. So little separating the two words, the two poles.

Asher.

Ashes.

Just one breath apart.

When Arin was born nineteen years ago, I cried and cried knowing he would die someday, not able to bear the fact I had brought this beautiful life into the world and one day he would be gone. Matt forced me to wrap my hand around the baby's limbs. "This is his arm," he told me. "This is his leg. This is real. He is here, alive, now." And I held those pulsing limbs in my hands and tried to not think of them vanishing.

Asher to Ashes. I can't bear the thought now, either.

Ash er

Ash es

Later my sister will tell me that as she held Asher, held ashes, in the hallway, she felt a bright current pass through both her arms, a pulsing, a vibration so strong she could barely hold on to the two charged things; she had to stand straight to hold herself together. Life and death coursing wild and hot through her body. But now I just see her standing tall, holding all of it with grace as I stumble

stumble stumble in her wake, leaking blood and milk, my own edges blurry . . .

. . .
ash/er/ash/es/ash/er/ash/es
dust to dust to dust

ARLENE: The Ehlers-Danlos side was obviously on my
   mother's side. She had this very milky-white, flawless
   skin that was very indicative of Ehlers-Danlos
   syndrome. Um, she lived until she was sixty-seven,
   although just weeks before she died, she had these
   huge bruises on her back and they were obviously
   mid-sized arteries that were spontaneously bursting.
   That happens with vascular EDS. Um, so she was — When
   I told a doctor about it, I was so angry with a doctor
   that she had, when I was trying to explain this, and
   the first thing he said to me, "Well, did anyone hit
   her?" And I said, "Well, for heaven's sake (laughs),
   you know, nothing like that; that's the farthest from
   anything that could be possible." So that was his
   first assumption, and um, then she died very suddenly.
   I had breakfast with her that morning, Friday the
   13th. I happened to be off of work that day, and we
   had breakfast together, and then ten minutes later,
   I took a telephone call, and then ten minutes later,
   she was dead on the sofa, and it was just that sudden.
   The same way my four brothers died after that, between
   1970 and '80. They talk about most people not living
   beyond their thirties and forties with vascular
   EDS, but you know, I just turned seventy—I'm telling
   the world (throws out her arms and laughs)—and my
   mother was sixty-seven and my brothers were mostly
   in their forties, one fifty-one, and my grandfather,
   thirty-eight, but all died the same way, and all
   thought to be sudden cardiac arrest.

Mom,

You stuck with NOFAW and its sister organizations about two years, longer than most of your projects. You had huge ambition, but an issue with follow-through. As soon as you came upon any stumbling blocks, hit any walls, you dropped the project at hand and were on to the next scheme.

The first thing you did when you had a fresh idea was order business cards; seeing that rectangle of stiff paper made your new calling more real for you. I found many of them after you died.

You and Dad started Mercury Marketing Direct after his company went bankrupt in the mid-'80s and the two of you launched a new direct mail marketing business together. I suggested Mercury in the name—I was heavily into mythology at the time, and thought Mercury would connote speed and power and communication, all good for advertising. MMD fizzled out, though, and Dad, at seventy, was hired by a hip ad agency in Chicago, where he became a much beloved and admired figure in HR. He was working there when you tried to kill him. Work became his refuge, his truest home.

After you disbanded NOFAW and your other organizations, you reached out to Dad. You never apologized to him. You never stopped believing he was hiding a fortune. But you were lonely, and you seemed to remember better times; you seemed ready to let him back into your life. You invited him to meet you at an Italian restaurant on Rush St. for dinner. He was cautiously ecstatic. He had missed you terribly.

The two of you never lived together again, but—other than times when you were having one of your episodes and were awful to him—you quickly resumed being one another's world. You talked every morning, saw each other almost every day. As always, you were worried about money, so Dad set you up as a recruiter, a head hunter, for the ad agency where he worked. You resurrected Mercury Marketing Direct for this endeavor, printing the same logo on your business cards, but using your maiden name so it wouldn't seem as if Dad was showing favoritism. He hired many of your clients; you ended up making more money than he did.

You ultimately gave up headhunting when you decided to move to San Diego. You were in the midst of a long, bad episode; if you wanted to hunt anyone's head, it was Dad's. You removed yourself, instead, seeking the geographic cure of California.

When you were around ten, you and your mother and two of your nine siblings—Rochelle and Mickey, the brother who poured milk in the mouth of your Betsy Wetsy doll, then plugged up the pee hole so the milk curdled and a maggot wriggled out between her lips—had your picture taken on what looks like the back of a train, an "Off To California" sign by your feet. Rochelle looks beautiful, her dark wavy hair pulled back from her pale face; Mickey looks like a bully, staring down the camera; your mom has a bit of a smirk on her matronly face, and you, sitting on a tall stool in the center, your face broad and Eastern European looking, your hair pulled back in braids, look happy, excited, as if you know California is your destiny, as if you know you'll be the only member in your family to actually move to California. As if you have no idea California is where your story will end, and not well.

DECEMBER 5, 2009

We caravan to the Oceanside harbor. I keep thinking the back of Larry's head in the car ahead of us is the back of my mom's head, hair cropped close, ears flaring at the same angle, and when I remember she doesn't have ears anymore, doesn't have a head, that all that is left of her head, her ears, the rest of her, is inside a wooden box inside a fancy looking bag on the floor of the car, I feel like I've been zapped by a cattle prod.

We pull up to the Dolphin Dock, which feels appropriate—my mom liked to think of herself as a dolphin when she swam—and walk down the rickety ramp in procession. It's a gray day, lots of clouds, the water beaten pewter. A sea lion bobs its head up, and it feels like a good sign to have one of her beloved "critters" here.

We gather in an oblong circle on the dock. Sue passes the yellow roses we asked her to pick up—our mom's favorite flower—so we're each holding one. Asher is wrapped against Michael's body with the long stretch of green cloth and tucked inside Michael's peacoat; I keep peeking over to make sure he isn't getting smothered.

I read "Meaning," the stately Czeslaw Milosz poem my mom had told us years ago she wanted to have read at her funeral. The poem asserts that everything will make sense upon death, and goes on to say that if everything doesn't make sense, there will be something of us that remains, some part of us that will protest this lack of meaning, even after death. My mom had added a few lines of her own at the end:

And then, in that new dimension,
We'll become whale riders
In the oceans of the universe.

So emblematic of her, thinking she could improve upon a Nobel-winning poet.

Elizabeth opens the simple wooden urn, untwists the tie that cinches the plastic bag within it.

"I need to touch it," she says, her voice almost a growl, the words coming from a deep, raw place. She digs into the ashes. Later she says her whole hand felt electric until we got back to our dad's house. She says, "I love you, Mom," and releases some of the ashes into the water. I dig my hand in, too; it feels impossible that this grit is all that's left of my mom, her eyes, her heart, her womb, her bones. I toss some ashes, a paler, softer gray than I had imagined, and watch them enter the water. It's so beautiful, the way some billow and bloom under the surface, like jellyfish, or a mushroom cloud, while others swirl on the surface like oil. We shake the rest of the bag out into the air—some of the ashes fly back at us, stick to our jackets, our hair, our lips. We laugh and cry all at once as we brush ourselves off, then take turns tossing our yellow roses into the water, some of us saying a few words, some of us casting our flower in silence. Light slices through the clouds like in a religious painting; the yellow roses are vibrant, so vibrant against the silver water as they slowly drift away.

Later in the day, Elizabeth, Michael, Asher, and I drive to my mom's house for the first time since her death—the first time for me and Elizabeth and Asher, at least; Michael was here earlier with Nancy and Jenn to try to clear out some bad energy. Just as we pull into her driveway, a giant crow—so big, it looks like a raven—swoops down close over the windshield. Elizabeth and I both say "Whoa" at the same time. A chill passes through me. When I look down, I see the odometer reads 666, which gives me a deeper chill, even though I don't believe in hell.

From here on out, every time I see a crow, I'll think of my mother, wonder whether the crow is her.

. . . .

We sit in the car a while longer, not ready to go inside. I try to eat the sandwich Michael and Elizabeth had picked up at the Sprouts deli while I waited in the car with the sleeping baby, but can only choke down a couple of bites of cucumber and hummus before I fold the rest back into its paper wrapper. Michael and Elizabeth aren't able to eat much of their sandwiches, either.

We get out of the car. Michael unlatches the car seat. Elizabeth and I hold hands in the driveway and look at each other, take a deep breath to give each other strength. It helps to know Nancy and Jenn had burned sage, had shaken rattles, had washed the mirrors with salt water, but I'm still scared to enter the house, as if my mom had killed herself here, too, and we're about to find her body.

Her arty wind chimes clink in the breeze as we pass, give an eerie soundtrack as we move down the walkway. She had painted the front door a dark brown to mask the splintering faded wood carved into a grid of raised squares, like a door of a small castle. She had done a lot of work on the house, stripping away the red flocked wallpaper, the deep red shag, turning it from what looked like a vampire bordello into a classy joint filled with art and light.

Now the air inside feels stale. Elizabeth and I keep holding hands, walking in slow motion as if something is going to jump out at us. And little things do jump to our attention—the books she had stacked against the door of the water heater, as if to block out fumes, a small dish of vitamins next to an open bottle of water by the sink, two thin brown dress socks crumpled on the floor. They, more than anything, move me; they, more than anything, bring back her living body, her living feet, her chaotic state of mind.

Each object in the house feels fraught with meaning; every object feels like a heartbreaking gesture of hope. People only buy things if they believe they're going to use them, if they believe they'll be alive awhile to use them. Each item of clothing in the closet feels wildly infused with the future, the promise of dinner dates, art openings, evenings at the opera. Each one now hangs empty.

We walk into the bathroom together, the mirror streaked with salt. Our reflections blur before us, ghostly. We are ghosts visiting the house of a ghost.

FOUR DEAD BROTHERS

ARLENE: Now, this is another big story for the cardiac
community to look at, and I am convinced that Dr.
Sheldon Pinnell, who told me to take high doses of
vitamin C when I had my genetic testing at Duke
University Medical School, and he was one of the major
researchers in the field, and he said take two to five
thousand milligrams of vitamin C. Well, I used to
bruise very easily; I mean, I would do this (touches
hand) and have a bruise, and since I've been taking
vitamin C, that doesn't happen, and since reading
Linus Pauling, actually after we began the filming
for this, I had only my own history to go by, knowing
vitamin C is so crucial to this issue, and when I
think of hospitals taking away people's vitamins, and
the keloid scarring which can happen—my mother had
abdominal surgery and had this huge, raised, pink,

whitish-looking scar that was really unusual, and I
had never heard the term "keloid scarring," but I know
Linus Pauling suggests that when people have surgery,
they be given vitamin C intravenously.

I don't think it's commonly known by most people how
important it is to the body; it's the building block
of our tissue, and 80 percent of our body is made up
of collagen. I mean, it's your skin, it's your organs,
it's your vascular system, it's your digestive system—
it's all made out of collagen. So knowing how to keep
that healthy is really important.

It is all about the sudden death of my four brothers.
All healthy, vital men. One died at a gas station
on New Year's Eve, gassing up his car, where he was
alive, ready to go out with his wife for the evening,
and the next minute he was on the ground, dead. That
was Leonard. My brother Harvey died at work; they
found him in the morning. Sheldon, also at work, was
an insurance broker and died at his desk, and Al, who
died in his sleep, was the only one who had an autopsy
and they found nothing wrong; they found his heart was
normal size, normal weight; they found there was no
plaque, no clot, no nothing. So when I told this to
Dr. Byer, who is another specialist in Ehlers-Danlos
syndrome—I went to an Ehlers-Danlos conference that
was held about five years ago in LA, shortly after I
moved to California—and he said that if, during the
autopsy, they had lifted the liver and looked at
the artery under the liver, that with Ehlers-Danlos
syndrome, that is the most common place to have a
rupture. If they had only known about vitamin C, I
mean, you know, they could still be alive today.

Mom,

The first time you went to the opera was with Eli. You were probably nineteen. You sat in the Lyric Opera House and felt a whole new world of majesty open to you, open within you. Nothing in your blue collar upbringing had prepared you for this. This was a different kind of electroshock therapy—your whole body electric, shocked into life.

You convinced Dad to buy season tickets during your courtship; you kept these season tickets most of your married life. When I was an infant, you dropped me and a babysitter off at Dad's office and would zip over during intermission to nurse me, racing back before the curtain opened again.

You ultimately found your way behind the curtain, yourself, serving as a supernumerary, the fancy opera word for "extra"—first at the Lyric, starting in 1992, and then later, after you moved to California, at the San Diego Opera. Your first production as a super was *Electra*; at the audition, the choreographer said she didn't see you as a slave; she thought you'd make a good high priestess. You wrote, "My debut was the Electra procession scene, carrying a bowl of dry ice above my head on a catwalk above the stage. It was the biggest forty-five-second thrill of my life." I had the chance to see your second production, *The Masked Ball*—my family was visiting Chicago; Arin was a toddler, and Dad drove around the city with him while Matt and I watched you glide about in your large-skirted gown with other party goers while the principals sang. It was a rush to see you look so graceful and elegant, like you were born to be on that stage. This was the year before your delusions started, so I was able to enjoy the performance without getting distracted by the many layers of fantasy and reality you came to inhabit.

You had amazing costumes as a super—for *Aida*, your whole body (at least all that was exposed) was painted blue. In several productions, you were dressed like royalty, the sort of dress you felt was your birthright.

I can't remember when you decided to put together an anthology of writings about opera, what the impulse was behind it (although there may be some clue in the introduction you drafted, which ends with "I should thank those few older 'regular' super women who have been so unwelcoming and rude to me over the years . . . I'll be thinking about them and their pre-adolescent behavior, only briefly, when I'm on my book tour.").

I helped you put a call for manuscripts in *Poets & Writers* magazine and you were deluged with submissions, some from well-known writers. I was too busy to help you with the anthology—I think you had expected me to do most of the work and were livid when I couldn't find a way to make myself more available. The anthology became too big a task for you alone—"I'm a little dyslexic," you often told me; "I can't handle so much paperwork"—so you let it go, all those poems and essays and short stories about opera conscripted into silence. After you died, I didn't know what to do with the box of writings, and ended up heaving it, heart heavy, into the recycling bin. Perhaps some of those poems have turned into paper towels or newsprint. Perhaps when someone lifts a paper cup to their lips, they kiss the ghost of Madama Butterfly.

You ultimately bowed out of the San Diego Opera because of the "pre-adolescent" women involved; you ended up bowing out of your work as a museum docent because you thought you were being undermined. It's possible you were asked to leave.

You decided to turn your docent experience into your own art presentations, which you pitched to upscale hotel chains and cruise lines—if any of them ever said yes, it could be a way for you to travel for free (and you loved to travel, taking Dad on cruises to Greece and Turkey and the Bahamas with your head-hunter money when you were well enough to enjoy his company). You envisioned Artful Conversations as virtual "tours" of art and architecture—slide shows, essentially—that you could give to travelers looking for a little cultural enrichment.

Part of your proposal read

> In addition to being a Museum Educator, I am a part time actor. I bring a down to earth approach which is not intimidating to the viewer, but fun and entertaining. My presentations have been referred to as:
> - Informative
> - Filled with wit and humor
> - Appreciated for revealing issues sometimes difficult to understand
> - Giving attendees a real handle on Contemporary Art to take away with them.
> - And much more.

Other than your supernumerary experience, the only work you'd done as a "part time actor" had been to awkwardly walk through a party scene in a made for TV movie filmed in San Diego—you didn't look at home in front the camera the way you had on the Lyric stage. The times I'd seen you docent, you had clearly gone off script and added your own questionable interpretations to each piece of art, gazing at the audience after each pronouncement as if you had just imparted some deep wisdom.

You decided you wanted "sacred architecture" to be part of your presentation; you wanted to weave together facts about the pyramids of Giza, Stonehenge, Machu Picchu, Chichen Itza, and, asynchronously, the Salk Institute in La Jolla, where you had also been a docent, and thought it would be good to experience some of the ancient sites first hand. You traveled to Egypt with a goddess-themed tour in 2006. The trip was supposed to be rapture, revelation, but when you called me a few days after you arrived in Cairo, you said a male housekeeper had drugged you and possibly sexually assaulted you (you had woken up in just a turtleneck, no bra. You had some itching; you worried about STDs).

I didn't want this to be true, but I didn't want to doubt you, either—all people who report sexual assault need to be taken seriously. I did my best to help—I passed along the number of the embassy; I convinced you to go to the hospital. I was relieved when all the tests came back negative.

Dad was behind it, you were certain. Dad and his son Jon, who had recently produced a series about Middle Eastern music for PBS; you assumed he had used his contacts, had put Dad in touch with the right people. You thought Dad and Jon were in cahoots, that Dad had paid for Jon's large house in the Malibu hills, that Dad was a closet misogynist, that he was sharing his vast secret fortune with his son and leaving his wife and daughters in the dust. You thought they had arranged to have you drugged and raped in Egypt; you imagined they had arranged to have you killed, that they were responsible for dropping a bottle from an overpass that hit your windshield shortly after you got back home, but you had outsmarted them; you had survived.

DECEMBER 28, 2009

My mom's death certificate arrives in my Redlands mailbox a couple of weeks after my sister leaves town, after I've weeded through all my mom's stuff, after we've had an estate sale company arrange to sell everything we don't want to keep. We've been waiting for the certificate so we can take care of business—shut off her cable, access her bank accounts, transfer the title of her car. I find myself a little scared of the stiff paper inside the manila envelope, but I slide it out, let its flimsy weight settle in my hands. I can barely look at my mom's name. I focus, instead, on the image of the native woman at the center of the page, part of the watermarked seal for the County of Los Angeles, focus on the light radiating from her head.

124. Describe How Injury Occurred (Events which resulted in injury)

HANGING BY ELECTRIC CORD FROM PIPE

The words "cord" and "pipe" make the act feel more stark. More real. The syllables lodge themselves deep in my body.

125. Location of Injury (street and number, or location, and city and ZIP)

1000 EL CENTRO STREET, SOUTH PASADENA, CA 91030

We knew she had hanged herself in a random parking garage, but until now had no idea what sort of establishment the garage served—a medical building, perhaps a restaurant. Now, an actual address. I plug it into my computer, and the result forces a sharp laugh from my lungs, startling Asher off my breast.

Golden Oaks Luxury Apartments.

I find myself strangely comforted as I click around the website of Golden Oaks, which turns out to be apartments for seniors; this is so much better, more fitting, than if the address had revealed a Walmart or a Starbucks or some generic office building.

My mom had been on a delusional quest for gold, for luxury, for the last sixteen years. It appears she had finally found it.

ARLENE: It's just remarkable that there hasn't been more
stressing on vitamin C. I mean certainly Dr. Pinnell
told me to take it when I had my genetic test, my
positive test for vascular Ehlers-Danlos syndrome,
and it just made a world of difference in the way
I feel. So each of these vital, healthy men died of
what was thought to be sudden cardiac death. Now,
there are 310,000 sudden cardiac deaths in America
every year. I can't believe that many of them aren't
connected to vascular EDS. So vitamin C is such a
simple thing to take and especially after reading
Linus Pauling's book, I am more and more convinced
that my own personal experience was spot-on with my
bruisability just almost disappearing. So it's an
important message to get out there, and I mean, this
is my mission in making this video, this documentary.
I think it has the potential to save lives and to stop
a lot of misdiagnoses that go on in this country and
around the world. So I fully feel that the spirits of
my family have propelled me to do this documentary, to
tell this story, to try to educate doctors, emergency
rooms, nurses, the lay public, that there are such
simple things to do to manage these problems. High
carbohydrates—not a high diet, I mean, you don't have
to get obese.

Mom,

You never did give an Artful Conversations talk, but you recycled the name for your nascent author escort service. After I told you that people were employed to drive authors to and from events on their book tours, that Michael Chabon's mom had driven me around on one of my tours in the Bay Area, you wanted in on the action.

You saw yourself as a book publicist long before I had a book out. As I was digging through your papers, I found a letter you had sent to Golden Books, along with a collection of my juvenilia, when I was eight years old. "You would be wise to snatch up this young talent," you trumpeted. An editor had responded, thanking you for the submission, saying it wasn't right for Golden Books, but she hoped I would keep writing—my first positive rejection letter (the likes of which I would be heartened by a couple of decades later when I started to send my work out, myself). You, undeterred, wrote back to the editor, warning her in playful yet firm language that one day she would regret her decision.

As much as I appreciated your support, your publicity schemes embarrassed me over the years. I cringe to think of how the *New York Times* or the *Washington Post* must have reacted to your passionate and creatively punctuated letters, urging them to review me or excoriating them for not doing so. I doubt I ever would have gotten any closer to Oprah just because you sent numerous entreaties on my behalf. I would tell you this was the job for professionals, that I would be taken less seriously when you tried to promote me, and you would bristle, offended I considered your efforts amateurish. "Besides," you would say, "sometimes personal is better than professional. It will stand out more." That's exactly what I was afraid of.

When my novel *Self Storage* came out in hardcover, the dust jacket featured a red bra stuffed inside a mason jar. You jumped on that immediately, purchasing a red bra (slightly more orange than the one in the image), folding it into a mason jar, and affixing the Starbucks logo to the side with scotch tape before sending it to their corporate office. "Books in Starbucks do well," you said. "They could give bras away with it as a promotion." My head spun trying to imagine the logistics of such a campaign, but you weren't tied to the mundanities of reality, even when you weren't having one of your episodes. I also found copies of letters you had written to Steven Spielberg and Nora Ephron, pitching my first book, *Fruitflesh: Seeds of Inspiration for Women Who Write,* as the next animated hit. Somehow you thought that a book full of writing exercises would make a great cartoon. You asked Steven and Nora to imagine fruits "sensually interacting with one another." I wish I could have stepped inside your brain to see what you had been visualizing.

Some of your publicity ideas did bear fruit. You started a book club at the Oceanside Museum of Art, primarily to create a venue to promote my novels. You made calls that led to both reviews and interviews in the San Diego area media, as well as speaking engagements in libraries and at political functions. And you beamed at all of these events, ever the proud mama, unless I said something you weren't happy with, and then I had to try not to be thrown off by the daggers shooting from your eyes.

After serving as the fundraising chair for the local Democratic club, you decided to turn fundraising into a way to make money, yourself. You pictured a line of nutritional bars that could be sold door to door to raise money for different organizations, a healthy alternative to Girl Scout cookies and Sees chocolates.

You used swaths of your "Art of Misdiagnosis" triptych paintings as background for the labels you had mocked up; you imagined you could use these nutritional bars to raise awareness and money for both the American Porphyria Foundation and the Ehlers-Danlos National Foundation, among other organizations.

You toured different Southern California factories that manufactured nutritional bars—I helped you taste-test some of them and was especially fond of a raw bar with a cashew and sesame base (I can still taste it now). You never found the perfect product, but you kept looking.

You were searching in other ways, too. You got involved in Kabbalah around this time, and it was like a dose of magic, like you had finally found the medicine you needed—the deepest, most profound medicine. You started to look at yourself and others with more compassion. You started trying to let go of old hurts, to let go of ego. You sometimes proselytized a bit, sometimes got a little overbearing with your spirit talk, but we didn't mind—it was vastly preferable to your usual harangues and accusations. *This is it,* we thought. *She's better now. She found the cure.*

How easily we fooled ourselves.

You just couldn't let well enough be, a common theme. After your frenzy of abstract painting, you weren't able to let that be its own gift, to be grateful for the creative outpouring. It had to be recognized, monetized. You contacted the curator at the Museum of Contemporary Art in Chicago where you had been a docent and suggested they mount a "40 Day Retrospective" of your work. It wasn't enough that you had reconnected with your estranged family through your paintings—in your heart, if not in the world. It wasn't enough that you discovered you could paint. You wanted to be celebrated as the next Grandma Moses.

The same thing happened with Kabbalah. The sense of peace and spiritual connection it offered wasn't enough. You set up a meeting with the head of the Kabbalah Centre Los Angeles, where Madonna studied, and proposed that you and he work together to create Kabbalah Bars as an off-shoot of Good for You Nutrition. When the director wasn't amenable to this idea, you soured on Kabbalah, itself. You stopped your exploration, your earnest quest for knowledge and growth.

Soon, you were convinced Dad was trying to sabotage your business. When you visited the company that was going to help you with distribution, you thought you saw the name of one of Dad's former business associates on the visitor list; you were sure Dad had sent him to undermine you. Then you were sure the business partner you had enlisted was trying to undermine you, too. It wasn't long before you washed your hands of the whole business. "'Good for You'?" you'd mutter. "More like 'Good for Nothing.'"

JANUARY, 2010–MARCH 15, 2010

Michael and I have been looking at real estate on and off over the past year; we took a break right before our wedding and haven't resumed until now. The cat pee smell of the house is getting to us again, plus the dishwasher makes the whole house shake, and the sewer has a nasty habit of flooding the side yard and sometimes bubbling up the shower drain. Plus, grief has become synonymous with this address, has seeped into the very walls of the place. Post-traumatic torpor has led us to neglect the back yard, and the weeds have grown taller than our heads. It is remarkable to watch nature take over, to see what entropy spawns, life growing lush and unchecked around us as we sit, numb, on the couch, but we receive a nasty letter from the "Buena Vista Beautification Committee"—likely a solitary neighbor hiding under the first person plural—threatening to report us to the city if we don't mow everything down.

We decide to look in Riverside after Matt insists Hannah move in with him so he can oversee her shift to a new school—a request that guts me; haven't I lost enough? Michael works in Riverside; as much as we like Redlands, nothing is keeping us here now, and life would be easier for Michael without a long commute. The night we look at an eccentric mountain lodge plunked into the middle of town, a place at the furthest reaches of our budget, a place with an abundance of fireplaces and a sunken living room and funky photo murals on several walls, I dream my mom left a note in its dated '80s kitchen. I read her familiar handwriting as I lean against the pine cabinets, the white tile countertop dotted with brown flowers.

"That was not me," the letter says. "The woman who killed herself—that was not the real me."

I can hear my mom speaking in my head as I read, and it is the first time I've heard her true voice—calm, reassuring, not strained with paranoia—in a long, long while.

I wake knowing we need to buy the house.

Michael and Asher and I continue to live in Redlands while we renovate the new place. One day when Hannah is over, a little before Asher turns four months old, we get a call from Riverside Community Hospital. Michael's mom Jette has been brought to the ER, but they can't tell us her condition over the phone. Michael doesn't take the news seriously—his mom often ends up in the ER seeking pain medication—but Hannah knows something is wrong, very wrong. Hannah has really stepped up since my mom's death; she's been very kind, very helpful, for which I'm deeply grateful.

"You should go," she tells Michael.

And when he does go and finds his mom on life support, Hannah suggests we go there, too. She and I sit outside the ER on a concrete bench; Hannah stays with her baby brother whenever I go inside to check on Michael, who is teary and shaken. I find myself trying to not breathe too deeply, not wanting to take hospital air into my lungs. I have become a germaphobe since my mom's death—every time we go out into the world, I am afraid someone will breathe a virus or bacteria onto Asher his new immune system won't be able to handle.

And it's not just germs—I've started to see catastrophe everywhere. Every time I walk through a doorway, I worry I'll trip and crack Asher's skull like an eggshell against the doorframe. Intrusive thoughts like "These are the stairs I'll fall down while I'm holding him and he'll break his neck" and "This is the tub he'll drown in" barrel into my head multiple times a day. I try to not see them as prophesies. I try to stay present, to just enjoy Asher's babyhood, but the whole world feels rife with potential peril.

I recently told a friend about these obsessive thoughts, scared she'd think I was losing my mind—I was starting to worry about my mental health, myself—but she said, "It's normal. It's normal to be hyper-vigilant when you've been sideswiped." It gives me a measure of relief to know this is a common reaction to unexpected loss. And now Michael and his sister, who drives out from LA, make the decision to turn off Jette's life support, and we have yet another unexpected loss to face.

GAYLE BRANDEIS, Daughter/Author.

[Gayle is sitting in front of *The Art of Misdiagnosis*,
panel 3, looking puffy with pregnancy—even her neck looks
puffy—wearing a dusky lavender tunic.]

GAYLE: Well, my mom had such a profound influence on me when
I was young, as a writer and as a budding activist,
because I would see her write what she called poison-pen
letters if she was ever upset about anything, and this
could be something minor, such as, you know, a hair in
her soup. I don't know if that ever actually happened,
but something along those lines. She would write to the
restaurant and often get a free meal in the process, and
so I would see that if you're upset about something, you
raise your voice, you use your voice, and you let them
know that this thing upset you. If you see injustice you
raise your voice, you let them know; if you see something
that needs to change . . . Um, she was involved in the
safety council at my elementary school and she was able
to (clears throat) excuse me, get a stop light put into
a dangerous intersection near my school where there had
been a lot of accidents, and through a letter-writing
campaign, she and other mothers were able to make it
a safer intersection, and they also were able to, at
my mom's organization, get guns and ammunition out of
our local Kmart, and this was decades before Michael
Moore did that in his film *Bowling for Columbine*, and I
watched her do these things and could see how a singular
voice could make a real difference in the world and how
the written word could make a real difference, and how
when you join voices together, it can make even more of
a difference.

Mom,

I don't know where all your ambition and creativity came from. You grew up in a home where art wasn't valued, where education wasn't valued, where your family would eat the huge Sunday dinners your mom had prepared—pot roast your father had butchered in his little grocery store, kasha, solid Jewish food—mostly in silence.

I was groomed for a creative life, but you—you had to build it all from scratch. You were a self-made woman, and you made and remade yourself over and over again.

Another thing you pursued later in life was a senior modeling career. You had been a model when you were young, wearing structured dresses with cinched belts that accentuated the twenty-three-inch waist you had been so proud of when you were a model, your "little pinched-in waist," as you liked to call it. You walked around a special parlor at Blums Vogue, displaying couture for women who could afford the personal shopping service; you used the posture you had learned at the Patricia Stevens Finishing School in downtown Chicago, where you strode across rooms with books stacked on your head, where you learned to fence. I'm not sure how fencing is supposed to "finish" a girl, but I loved seeing the silver foil you kept in the coat closet, its slender blade speaking of your youth, its jab of promise.

You never let go of that desire to be seen, admired, exalted for your bearing and beauty. After you died, I found a letter you had written to Ronald Lauder, chairman of Clinique Labs, suggesting he use you in an advertising campaign:

Dear Mr. Lauder,

I'd like to approach you with the idea of being your Clinique "dramatically different moisturizing lotion" spokesperson.

I have used that product somewhere between 32 and 35 years.
I'm not sure when it first came on the market, but I've been using
it always since its availability.

An ad campaign "65 and Glowing" for print and commercials
would be wonderful, using me, of course.

People always comment on my beautiful skin, my best feature.
I credit genetics and your product.

I've included my model photographs, which have darkened some
in the printing process. My true skin tones are lighter and milkier.

I hope you'll consider this suggestion.

Sincerely,
Arlene Baylen Brandeis

The photographs you had prepared that year to go after senior modeling and Central Casting extras jobs show you in various outfits, in various stilted poses. In your head shot on the front of the composite, you appear to be smirking; in one of three pictures on the back, you wear a red short-sleeved turtleneck, the one from the coroner's bag, and are laughing uncomfortably; in another, you stand at an angle to the camera, a black scarf knotted around your neck, a loop of pearls arcing between it and your asymmetrical black blouse. You seem to be touching your bottom with your right hand, an unconscious movement you often performed as you walked, as if checking your panty line. You somehow look most comfortable in the picture in the center, where you're dressed as the lady in waiting to the Spanish queen in the San Diego Opera production of *Don Carlo*, looking very regal yourself in a severe black gown with a black mantilla and a giant white ruffled collar that resembles a car's air filter. It's the only photo where your bearing doesn't look forced and stiff. You may have been a supernumerary, but in your mind, you were always the star. You insisted your daughters were stars, too, although I think you saw us more as moons, objects that orbited around you, reflecting shards of your brilliance.

APRIL 2010–AUGUST 2013

We move into our new house about a month after Jette dies, after we've done some remodeling, after we've gone on a disastrous book tour for *My Life with the Lincolns,* my novel that came out a day after Jette's death—a book tour during which I sobbed at one reading and ended up in the ER with one of my vomiting episodes after another, a book tour during which Michael walked into an empty classroom as I was giving one of my college talks and wrote, "My mother died two weeks ago and I still cry every day" on a white board with a fumey dry-erase marker.

Both of us are still shellshocked.

I am not writing much, if at all, but I tell myself I am learning about revision through renovation. Tearing rooms down to their studs, moving walls around to make the space more usable, choosing sustainable materials, updating switch plates and doorknobs and pendant lights—all of these things feel applicable to writing. Still, my lack of real writing has left me with a gnawing, growing sense of guilt and unease. I hire a babysitter to come a few mornings a week so I can attempt to seriously dive back into the world of words.

I've been wanting to write about my mom for years, but she had asked me to not write about her while she was alive. Now that I have that freedom, I freeze. *Be gentle with yourself,* my friends and family tell me, *don't expect too much of yourself right now; maybe it's too soon to write about her.* I try to heed this advice, but my lack of any substantial writing makes me feel like a failure. I force myself to write little bits about her, although I can only approach her death sideways—it's too hard to face it head-on. I write short fragments of a novel. Mostly, I use my babysitting time to respond to my online students' work and watch the blue jays dart in and out of the wisteria vines outside the window and futz around Facebook, "liking" things without having the energy to comment or post any updates of my own. My limbs feel full of wet cement; my brain, too. I feel that way even more so when Michael is home.

Without realizing it was happening, Michael and I have started to quietly loathe one another. I feel drained by his presence, by the heavy cloud of grief that surrounds him. When he comes home, my heart sinks. I've started to see him as weak, like his mom; I later learn he's started to see me as selfish, like mine. We glare at each other over dinner; we grow snippy with one another; we don't talk about what's pulling us apart.

We continue on this miserable path of denial for a couple of years. Not every second is torturous, of course; we garden and cook together; we run around the house and make sofa cushion forts and sing silly songs with Asher; we share blessed moments of laughter and affection. But we also fall into lots of seething silence, give each other lots of nasty side glances, and, between the two of us, we keep having lots of medical emergencies. Michael comes down with double vision, migraines, gallbladder attacks, kidney stones. I start to have more frequent episodes of pain and vomiting; they come every couple of months now, and are so bad, I end up having nasogastric tubes shoved up my nose and down my throat, something I hadn't needed before in my many visits to the ER. Doctors still can't figure out what's going on. Our bodies acknowledge we're falling apart even if our conscious minds deny it.

To add to this list of emergencies, my dad breaks his hip in 2012. When he is done with rehab, Michael and I move him to an assisted living place in Riverside so he'll be closer to us. After he graduates from a wheelchair to a walker, we move him to Olive Grove, which has more of an independent living focus, although care, which he still needs, is available. An apartment complex named Golden Oaks, the same name as the building where my mom ended her life, is one block away. I hate driving past it. The first time I saw the sign for Golden Oaks, I lost my breath; other times, the name makes me cringe so hard, my muscles cramp. When we first considered moving my dad, I wondered how I would survive seeing this sign on a regular basis. Over time, it has gotten a bit easier; seeing the name spelled out has become a homeopathic remedy of sorts—taken in small doses, the words "Golden Oaks" have less power to wreck me.

But I'm a wreck in other ways.

I enter a charged long distance communication with a writer I admire who lives on the other side of the country, a man old enough to move into Olive Grove, where the minimum age is sixty-two, although I can't imagine him inside those walls. It's hard to imagine him contained within any walls, his boundless sense of adventure such a contrast to the energy suck Michael has become. And this man flatters me—oh, how he flatters me. He calls me beautiful and brilliant; he says he's intoxicated by me. And I lap it up. I'm starved for it. I'm deeply intoxicated by him, myself; I charge toward him like a freight train. When Michael discovers our e-mails, he's understanding at first, and he and I try to work through the situation together, but when I continue to reach out to this man, Michael throws a punch through our hollow core bedroom door, bloodying his knuckles, terrifying me. Even then, I can't seem to stop. I've become an addict seeking a fix, craving that good dopamine rush after months and months of stagnation and stress. I feel more seen and heard and alive than I have in years.

Michael and I decide upon a trial separation and I arrange to stay in the guest suite at my dad's retirement community. Olive Grove seems like the ideal place to catch my bearings, figure out my next step.

Once I land in the apartment with its musty fake flower arrangements and its big wooden console TV, I can breathe more fully than I've been able to in ages. The rooms aren't buzzing with conflict. The walls are empty of history—at least my own. I can crawl under the cabbage-rose bedspread and know no one will be seething next to me. I love having my dad nearby. And on the days

Asher is here with me, he loves the place, too—the couch has become a great mountain for his action figures to climb, and there are many long hallways to explore. The residents generally smile as Asher runs past them in their walkers and wheelchairs and motorized scooters, seemingly grateful for the burst of youth he brings to the place. And I feel suddenly young and vibrant, myself, thankful for my strong and sturdy limbs, my freedom of movement. Being here reminds me these things won't last forever.

[BUZZ AND ELIZABETH sit together on the patio.]

BUZZ: The fact that Arlene has pulled this together, you know, and out of the need to spread the word, about the diseases Ehlers-Danlos and porphyria, is a remarkable thing, because, as Arlene says (Elizabeth sniffs loudly), it's part of the six thousand or so rare diseases that she feels that these two diseases don't belong there, because they're not as rare as people think (Elizabeth sniffs again). They're just rarely diagnosed properly. (Elizabeth says mmmhmmm, noncommittally) So to do this and be as passionate about it and to drive it as she has is a remarkable thing, because it could affect the lives of a lot of people (Elizabeth sniffs) who don't know otherwise, you know, how to handle these diseases. To spread the word to the medical community, I think is a terrific idea (Elizabeth says mmmhmmm and looks down), and to see the passion and the energy that she's been putting into it is remarkable.

ELIZABETH: The artistic expression in this project as well has been such a positive kind of project, taking elements that have been painful and difficult and confusing from her past and the family's past and kind of transforming that into a proactive and positive kind of force, um, is really quite amazing, that you know, she's been able to harness the pain of the past in such a positive way.

Mom,

In many ways, your documentary was a synthesis of your other endeavors—you were able to perform, like you did as a supernumerary, but this time, you were the diva, the one anchoring the show. You were able to talk about art the way you did as a docent, the way you wanted to do through Artful Conversations, but this time with your own paintings. You were able to raise awareness and money (at least that was the plan) the way you hoped to through Good for You Fundraising, but this time in a more personal way. You were able to work toward social change, the way you did with NOFAW, but without having to lobby Congress.

The Art of Misdiagnosis was a mix of vanity and philanthropy, a perfect amalgamation of you, and even though the whole process was plagued by your paranoia, even though it made your daughters' skin crawl, it came closer to completion than any other project you had started. You became a filmmaker at seventy, with no prior experience. It's quite amazing, really. I have to admire your vision, your follow-through. You wanted to make a film, and you did.

Celia's name appears in my inbox and my heart does a happy flip. Other than a brief visit in New York about ten years ago, I haven't seen Celia since she was my roommate in Bali, haven't heard from her in ages. Celia is going to be in Southern California visiting friends, she writes. She saw my essay in the *Rumpus* about my mom's suicide—the first piece of writing where I directly addressed her death—and is wondering if we might get together.

I desperately want to see Celia, but life has me off kilter and overwhelmed. I'm still settling in to my new post-Olive Grove bungalow and grappling with the fact that the house we own—where Michael still lives—has just been burglarized. Michael is out of town and I've had to deal with all the insurance and police reports and clean up. The worst part was seeing Asher's drawers yanked out of his dresser, his little clothes strewn on the floor. It doesn't help matters that the writer I'd been pining for broke my heart after a five day vacation together and I'm reeling, in a state of despair. I think of my mom's notes about the second season of grief: "We may hope for the wrong things." I don't know what to hope for anymore.

By the time I finally write back, Celia's almost ready to leave for the Bay Area.

"I'd love to give you a healing session as a wedding present if you have time," she writes; she had read about my new marriage in my essay.

"My husband and I are actually separated now," I tell her. I could use that healing more than ever.

I juggle some things on my calendar so I can drive out to San Diego to see Celia before she leaves town. As soon as I find her friend's house and she walks toward me, time folds in upon itself. Her soft British accent brings me right back to Bali, to black rice pudding for breakfast and the jangle of gamelan music and funeral processions running zig zag through the streets to outfox the demons who can't turn corners.

Celia's hair is now a pale coral orange—"I have help," she smiles when I remark upon it; my hair is threaded with white. Both of our faces show signs of the two decades that have passed, but I would never guess she is almost seventy, twenty-five years older than me. We are still ourselves, still the same women who whispered to each other through mosquito netting so many years ago.

Celia heats up some mung bean soup she had prepared the night before, an ayurvedic soup golden with turmeric. She slices up radishes and tomatoes and celery for a simple salad, douses them with olive oil and lemon. She toasts some bread in the oven, fries up some daikon, grabs a little pot of roasted garlic. We eat our lunch, delicious, outside in the lovely backyard garden, laundry draped over the backs of our chairs to dry in the sun, and we catch up on our lives.

"You've had so much to deal with," Celia says, and the concern on her face makes me realize that yes, yes I have. Maybe I shouldn't feel so guilty about being so upset lately—feeling weak, feeling like I don't know anything about life or love; feeling like I don't know anything at all. I think back to when I graduated from the University of Redlands in 1990, five months pregnant. My dad had asked me what I had learned in college, and I imagine he was expecting me to say something about literary theory or the like, but I told him, "I've learned three things: stay in the moment, keep my senses open, and don't take myself too seriously." I had been so sure at the time that I had learned everything I ever needed to know, that if I could only remember those three things, I'd be happy the rest of my life.

We drive out to the park her friend recommends, by the harbor. As we pull into the lot, my mind takes me up the coast to the harbor in Oceanside where we released my mom's ashes. We find a stretch of grass that seems fairly quiet, and Celia lays out a shawl for me to lie down upon, my purse as a pillow. I settle onto the fabric, the grass crackling beneath it.

I imagine we're going to focus on my belly, the way we did in Bali, the site of so much illness and stress, especially lately, but her hands keep being pulled like magnets over my chest.

"What's going on here?" she asks, and I find myself aware of a constriction I hadn't noticed before, or maybe have grown so used to, I don't notice any more. I inhale and my ribs contract, as if they don't want me to take a deep breath.

"Wow," I say. "I had no idea my chest was so tight."

"How would you describe it as an image?" she asks, and a board surfaces in my head, in my chest, a heavy gray board set firmly over my heart, weathered like driftwood but solid as slate. The board I had erected against my husband, against my own grief. Somehow I had been able to open my heart recklessly, lavishly, to this other man, but I had kept it closed off to myself. Her hand stays there, sending light and heat, and I can feel that board start to soften, can feel the pain and love I've trapped beneath it start to pulse and breathe as tears start to stream.

We don't have much time—I have to race back to Riverside soon to pick up Asher at preschool—but Celia packs our hour with one profound revelation after another, saying things like, "Your mother claimed ownership over your body; it's time to take it back," and, "You had a contract with your mom—you need to identify it so you can break it." She tells me that part of this contract was colluding with my mom over my illness as a teenager, that pretending to be sick is how I was able to survive.

"Your mother is still hovering around you," she tells me, and part of me is skeptical about this, about such things being possible, but the trees above us are full of crows. I think of the crow that swooped over our windshield at my mom's house. I think of the time I felt my mom's ghost hand on my shoulder.

Celia puts her hand on my left shoulder just as I am thinking about this. "She's right here," she says, sending shivers through my whole body. "You've been carrying her on this shoulder all your life." That shoulder has always been lower than the other one; my shirts tend to slip off on that side, *Flashdance* style. "It was part of your contract with her."

My hands and feet start to tingle.

"I think I'm hyperventilating," I tell her, remembering a time shortly before I left my first marriage when I was curled on our bed, crying so hard, I hyperventilated; crying so hard, I couldn't move my tingling hands.

"I think you know what you want to do and you're just scared to tell me," Matt had said, and he was right, he was so right—I knew I wanted to leave, but I couldn't admit it out loud to him yet; all I could do was sob my body into uselessness.

"People often experience tingling during a healing," Celia tells me. "It's energy being activated."

Breathe into it, I tell myself. Don't be so afraid. Don't knock her away this time. Celia's hand is still on my shoulder, sending warmth that radiates all the way down to my hips.

"What is it you want to say to your mom?" she asks, and I want to say something loving and forgiving, but the words that come barreling out of me, straight from my gut, words I had never thought to say before, are "How dare you."

"Yes," says Celia, and the tears pour and the same words keep coming out of me, louder and stronger each time. People are walking by now—I can hear them on the grass—but I don't care. I keep saying, over and over again, "How dare you. How Dare You. HOW DARE YOU?!" and Celia keeps saying, "Yes," encouraging me to let it out, to get it all out.

The words finally stop. I lie on the shawl breathing heavily, my entire body tingling now.

"It's time to let her go," Celia says quietly. "It's time to return to your true nature." She asks me to imagine I'm holding a knife, that I should use it to cut the invisible umbilical cord that still ties me to my mom. I start to plunge the knife toward my own belly—a hara-kiri of sorts—but then she clarifies that I should sweep it over the front of my body, slicing the knife above all the chakras. I feel an especially deep tug as my hand travels over my pelvis, severing my mother from places she never should have been.

When I am ready, Celia helps me up and hugs me back into the world.

"Thank you," I tell her, but the words don't feel strong enough. How can you thank someone for softening the board over your heart? For helping release a burden you've carried all your life? For resurfacing just when you need her? For saving you again, almost twenty-four years after she saved you the first time?

I don't have the same youthful hubris I did when I thought three aphorisms would spare me from sadness. I know I am not healed forever, absolved from pain for the rest of my life; I know I will still grieve for my mom, that my heart will still try to protect itself. But when I turn my head, I am stunned by the ocean; it looks more beautiful than ever, specks of my mom glinting in the waves.

GAYLE: I'm so proud of my mom, that she has taken the
pain of her family, the sadness of her family, that
she's transforming it in a way that's creative
and proactive, and that she's using that pain to
move forward and help others, and I think that's a
beautiful thing and something that I admire deeply.
Um, it is very, you know, ballsy of her to take on the
medical establishment, but I love that she's trusting
her instinct and following through with them, and
hopefully they'll listen.

Um, as for my place within it (looks off to side and
lets out a sharp exhale), that's hard to say because I
think so much of my life has been trying to see myself
as a healthy person and not identify so much with
illness, because I did that a lot when I was younger,
where illness became my identity to an unhealthy
extent, and so for my own personal well-being, I
needed to step away from that and just see myself
as a healthy individual, a healthy woman, and so
the medical issues aren't things I feel personally
compelled to go out there and fight for, um, but I'm
grateful that my mom is doing it.

Mom,

When you died, you were almost done with *The Art of Misdiagnosis*—everything was in place but the audio, which needed to be "normalized" (a word that I had trouble associating with you). I got in touch with the producer and sound guy you had hired after you broke things off with your original production team, and arranged to have the work completed posthumously. We didn't know what we'd do with the documentary when it was ready, but we knew how important the project was to you, and thought seeing it through would be the best way to honor you. The post-production audio specialist sent a sweet e-mail after he finished the work:

> When I first set out to clean up the audio I was uncertain as to whether the film could capture an audience due to its length & nature of content. After the dialogue was adjusted & Arlene's music choices were set in place I felt the whole dynamic of the project shift—no longer was it simply a documentary about two evasive medical conditions, but it was a door opening to a rich personal story.
>
> Art of Misdiagnosis is unlike any documentary I have ever seen because not only does it offer detailed science, but it brings you along for the journey & illustrates how a creative person like Arlene was able to channel her past into something positive. It is a beautiful example of the human ability to forge diamonds in the darkest times under immense pressure. I am proud to have been a part of this film's creation.

For all the complicated feelings I had about your project, it was good to see this response. The Ehlers-Danlos National Foundation also wrote a lovely tribute about you and your project, and included many photos of your paintings in their newsletter. Your work may not have changed emergency room procedure the way you had hoped, but it did touch people.

I continue to be grateful for your example, for the way your desire to make a difference has influenced my own desire to inspire change, a desire that helped me in the midst of my grief. Asher came down with pneumonia when he was three months old, and of course I went into a panic, worried I was going to lose him, too. Around this time, the women's peace organization CODEPINK asked me to write an action alert about a NATO airstrike in Afghanistan that had killed twelve members of one family, including six children. I had been writing the action alerts for CODEPINK for many years, but had planned to take a break from work after giving birth, a break that felt even more necessary after your death. Even so, I knew I needed to say yes to this project. Writing about such devastating and completely unnecessary loss helped put my own situation in perspective. Asher was going to be fine, our doctor had assured us; he had access to good health care—he was being treated; he was improving. Families bombed by our drones weren't so lucky. I was grateful to be of service, to be able to give people concrete actions they could do to speak out against further drone attacks; it helped take me out of my own little bubble of grief and anxiety, helped connect me to the pain of the wider world. It reminded me that I didn't want to just sit around worrying about the danger of every little cord, every little crumb. I wanted to reach out again; like you, I wanted to make a difference, even when I was feeling lost.

I wasn't able to bring myself to watch your completed film until almost five years after you died. I was at a weekend women's writing retreat at St. Mary's Art Center in Virginia City, Nevada; the building had originally been built as a hospital for miners in 1873 and is supposedly one of the most haunted sites in the country. The three days away from mothering and other responsibilities seemed like a good opportunity to face you, to face what you had made, what you had done. When I popped the DVD in Asher's portable player and heard you say, "I fully feel that the spirits of my family have propelled me to do this documentary" through my headphones—the first time I had heard your voice out loud since you died—a sob ballooned in my chest, but I held it in and heaved silently, not wanting to startle the women writing in the quiet rooms around me. When your image appeared on the tiny screen, my eyes were so full, I saw you through water—wavy and spectral as any ghost. Once I blinked, there you were, alive and standing. You, speaking about illness as I sat in an old hospital. You, whose mental illness was never diagnosed; you, who may have killed yourself to escape what you feared was imminent institutionalization, visiting me in a place once used as an asylum.

I still don't know what to do with your film. All I can do for now is weave it into my own story, give you a chance to speak for yourself.

DECEMBER 2013

Michael and I start to tiptoe toward one another again. Our months apart have been good for us. We've each realized we needed to be alone to grow stronger as individuals, to face our grief on our own time, in our own space. His family offers to fly me out to Louisiana for Christmas, along with Michael and Asher, even though we're still technically separated, still not sure what the future will bring. I am nervous—his stepmother's large family is Southern, quite religious, quite conservative, and I worry that I will be lectured or shunned, that I will be hated for what happened to our marriage—but everyone ends up embracing me. They practice what they preach in the best way, showing me forgiveness, showing me love. We end up having a wonderful time, and maybe it's the home-distilled apple pie moonshine, but I start to open my heart to Michael again. I start to remember he is kind and loving and patient, and, now that we're not seeing each other through a lens of bitterness, a lot of fun to be with.

I fly from Louisiana to Chicago for a sister retreat with Elizabeth, a chance to reconnect with our hometown and meet with our mom's sister. Sylvia is ninety-two now, happy to show us how she, a former Vaudeville dancer, can still touch her toes; when we were kids, she used to show us how she could do the splits. Our mom had told us that when she was born, Sylvia had to miss her prom so she could stay home and take care of the younger kids; supposedly Sylvia had resented her for this her whole life. We ask our aunt about missing her prom, and she says no, that never happened. "I used to wake up half an hour early every day so I could strip your mom's crib," she tells us. She would take the wet clothes and diapers off our mom's little body, bathe her and clothe her without complaint so their mother could get some rest.

We ask Sylvia about other stories, the one about their father, our grandfather, witnessing the rape and murder of his pregnant mother in Russia at the hands of Cossacks. And Sylvia says no, she doesn't know anything about this, and no, she doesn't know anything about their father letting Al Capone's men store weapons under his market in exchange for protection. At first we wonder if maybe our grandmother had only told these stories to our mom, her youngest, her princess, her pet, maybe she hadn't opened up to her older children the same way, but we also have to face the possibility that all our mom's stories were fiction; that she had made every single one of them up.

Muriel Rukeyser famously wrote, "The Universe is made of stories, not of atoms"; if this is true, what happens when our own foundational stories are exploded, when everything we thought we knew is shattered into subatomic particles? Elizabeth and I are shaken but surprisingly okay with this fresh discombobulation. Maybe it doesn't mean we're lost. Maybe it means we're free.

[As credits roll, image of GAYLE moves to a small square in the upper-left corner.]

GAYLE: Well, I really hope that my mom opens people's eyes and I think this film has a great potential for doing that, for educating the public and for getting these diseases sort of into the common consciousness. Um, yeah, and my mom does that all the time in our lives; she is kind of, uh, diagnosing people from a distance (laughs), such as my fiancé and people like Bernadette Peters, who have very clear, uh, beautiful skin, and um, she's on a mission, she's driven, and I just love that she has that energy. She does feel compelled.

[Note: After ARLENE showed Gayle and Michael the rough cut of the film, she gave Michael a gift-wrapped, economy-size bottle of vitamin C to help him with the Ehlers-Danlos she was sure hadn't been diagnosed properly yet.]

GAYLE: I hope that my mom will continue to follow her instincts both creatively and as an activist, and I have no doubt that she will (laughs), but I look forward to seeing where it will take her next.

Elizabeth and her husband, Craig, are in town from Toronto; I meet them for lunch, along with my dad, Arin, Michael, and Asher, at the Salted Pig, a gastropub in downtown Riverside. Michael moved into my little bungalow last month and while we're still working on repairing trust, things are sweet between us.

There's not much I can eat on the pork-heavy menu as a vegetarian—even the popcorn is cooked in bacon fat—but the vegetable sides are amazing, and I haven't been able to eat much lately, anyway. My belly has been in fairly constant pain since December, and eating only makes it worse. I haven't had one of my episodes since I was hospitalized for a few days last August—no vomiting at all—but for the past several months, I've felt like I've been stuck in an extended episode, the violent pain from my usual attacks stretched into one long attenuated ache. My new gastroenterologist has just put me on a hard-core drug that requires four hours in the chemo lab every week, one that will shut down my immune system. I resisted this treatment, but she said it was the only way to avoid surgery. The strictures the CT scan found in my small intestine were dangerously close to obstruction; this was a last-ditch effort.

My doctor calls after my family has ordered our lunch. I walk over to a corner of the noisy restaurant, tuck myself against a wall and hold my hand over one ear so I can hear her.

"How are you feeling?" she asks me.

"I'm still having pain," I tell her, "but it's not too bad right now."

"Your new blood test came back positive for Crohn's," she says. It somehow always sounds like "Chrome's" in her mouth, something shiny and hard. She had assumed that Crohn's is what had caused the strictures, but I hadn't been convinced, not fully, my mom's insistence I didn't have Crohn's still strong within me. This call makes the diagnosis real. I look over at my family sitting at the long table made of reclaimed wood. What would my mom say if she were with them, alive, and I came back with this news? "You have the marker for high risk of complication," the doctor tells me.

"Interesting," I say, my forehead against the wall now. The music from the speaker system thumps into my skull. All these years of misdiagnosis, and I am back to my original diagnosis, the one my mom was so certain was wrong. I thank the doctor and return to my family.

"Is everything okay?" my dad asks.

"I have Crohn's disease," I say. "It's official."

He lifts his eyebrows.

"Weird," my sister says.

Then the food comes; our server sets my order before me— brussels sprouts tangled with kimchi and fennel; butternut squash roasted in brown butter, dotted with pomegranate seeds, dusted with peanut-butter powder. My mouth waters.

I don't yet know it's the last solid thing I'll eat for eleven days.

After lunch, Michael, Asher, and Arin take off, and I follow Elizabeth and Craig back to Olive Grove. Pain hits me in my dad's living room, doubles me over by the wooden chest he uses as a coffee table. I kneel on the tan carpet, lay my belly against my thighs. *I ate too much*, I tell myself; *this will pass. I will feel better soon*. My default still tends to be denial.

When Elizabeth and Craig are ready to head to LA for the night before they fly back to Toronto, I can barely stand. I crouch in the ancient elevator; crouch in a bed of pansies when we get to the parking lot.

"Can I drive you home?" my sister asks, concerned.

I shake my head, encourage her to hit the road before traffic gets too bad, but I can barely see straight as I head back to my house. I almost stop the car in the middle of a railroad crossing because I'm about to throw up. Somehow I press on, hold it in until I get to my bathroom, and then I can't stop.

At the emergency room, I tell the doctor my pain level is a nine, but it really feels more like an eleven. It takes a while for the nurse to hook me up to the IV and start the pain medicine, and I writhe around on the ER gurney, vomiting into a little kidney-shaped bowl, peeing my pants more each time I throw up. The CT scan shows an obstruction; they decide to admit me into the hospital for further observation. The pain medication finally kicks in, and I feel like I'm floating as they wheel me into the elevator.

I look up at my reflection in the mirrored elevator ceiling. My legs, bent together to one side, look like a mermaid's tail beneath the thin blanket; my dark hair fans around my head like I'm in water. I am floating, floating, floating right out of my skin.

I find myself chronicling my hospital stay over the next few days, posting jokey things like "Feeling some cognitive disconnect as I attempt to eat my liquid breakfast (vegetable broth, Italian ice, hot water) while watching 'Deep Fried Masters.' Damn, those deep-fried deviled eggs on a stick look tasty" and "In my fine tradition of wardrobe malfunctions, I appear to have gone through my entire surgical consultation with my right boob hanging out of my gown."

A friend who brings clean underwear tells me that when she visits, what she sees is different from how I present myself online—online, I offer a brave, funny face; in person, I'm shaky and tearful. I realize I need to share this part of my experience, too. I don't need to pretend to be a hero—I can let myself know hard feelings now, know them and give them voice.

> March 13: "My doctor told me I need to complain more, and
> I burst into tears. I'm way too good at acting as if everything
> is okay, as if pain is normal, as if I should just be able to push

through it without asking for help, even though here in the
hospital, I'm surrounded by any kind of help I could possibly
need. Working on claiming and voicing my own hard truths—
easier for me as a writer than a person in the world, sometimes."

March 17: "A belligerent, disoriented woman was moved into my
room during the night. I'm mustering all the compassion in my
thin blood that I can for her, all the patience; it's forcing me to
process a lot of stuff about my mom, and I'm trying to see this as
a good thing, a way to learn and grow. But I'm also remembering
what my doctor said about how I need to complain more, so if it
gets too much, I'll ask for another room . . ."

My posts are getting more comments than I can ever remember
receiving and I worry I am letting myself become the Sick Girl all
over again, gaining the spotlight through illness. This feels different from when I was a teenager, though. This feels very different. I
write about how scary it is to have a PIC line installed, watching on
an ultrasound screen as the tube snakes toward my heart; I write
about spilling pee all over myself as I try to move the collection con-
tainer off the toilet. When friends comment back, I know they see
me as I truly am, human and flawed and vulnerable and real. I can
show myself at my lowest and people are willing to meet me there.

Dear Mom,

As I was wheeled into surgery to remove several inches of obstructed intestine, I was carrying so many people with me—all my family, of course, plus friends who had dreamed about me, friends who had sent messages and flowers, friends who were helping with Asher, friends I hadn't ever met in person who were sending hope my way.

I know I was carrying you, too.

When the surgeons reopened my Caesarean incision, when they sliced out the part of my intestine that was scarred—in so many ways—when I was sick as a teenager, they sliced part of you out, too, the part that's lived in the darkest recess of my body, the place where so many silences have accumulated. Then they stitched the rims of gut together, trusting my body would fuse them back into a single channel, open now, but forever marked by its rupture.

Shortly after you died, Elizabeth's husband, Craig, marveled at how it was a story that had killed you, a story your brain had made up. Writing our story now is saving me. I'm writing my way toward a more honest, more vocal life; I'm writing my way out of my anger toward you, writing my way toward compassion, toward admiration. I'm writing my way into feeling proud to be your daughter.

You would be so proud of your grandkids, Mom. I was surprised and grateful to discover the treasury bonds you had left for Arin and Hannah and Elizabeth's daughter Mo in your safety deposit box. They have used them well. Hannah got her GED, scored a perfect 800 on her verbal SATs, and moved to New York to become a standup comedian. She flew there having no idea where she'd live or how she'd support herself, and your generosity made it possible for her to get settled there, to create the life she'd dreamed of when she was camped out on our couch. Arin used the money to further his competitive cycling career, buying new bikes, taking three months to cycle across the country with his best friend. It fills my heart to see them both pursue their passions—something you cultivated in me; a legacy that lives on in them. I'm eager to see what Asher's long-term passions will be—so far, they've been trains and kitties and Legos and super heroes. And words. He loves words. He's such a sweetheart, Mom, such a light. You would have been wrapped around his pudgy little finger. I have to admit, sometimes Michael and I feel a sense of relief that Asher doesn't have to grow up surrounded by your and Jette's chaos, but more often than not, we feel sad that you don't know this beautiful boy.

Grief is such a strange process, so much more fluid than I ever could have guessed. Even more fluid than the grief map I found in your voice—the seasons come and go in strange order; I have moments where I feel I've reached season four, the creation of a compassionate heart, the opening to a larger story, but sometimes a scent or snippet of song or some other unexpected trigger will take me right back to the shock of the first season. Before you died, I imagined grief was a fixed thing; I thought it would be like carrying a bag of wet sand around in my heart all the time. Unyielding. Unrelenting. I thought that because of the way you grieved your mom; every time you talked about her, you cried horrible, gut-wrenching tears. Decade upon decade upon decade. I imagined there was no chance of healing, no chance of processing; grief just sat there, a bag of wet sand in your chest. And sometimes it does feel that way. I do always carry its weight. But its weight changes. Wet sand becomes a nest of wasps becomes water becomes anvil becomes a delicate soap bubble, iridescence swirling across its skin.

I'll always have questions for you. I'll always want to know why you left us the way you did. I'll always wish I could fill in the blanks about your life. But writing to you has helped me gain some level of acceptance, some modicum of peace. On the fourth anniversary of your death, Dad said, "She did what was best for her. It wasn't best for us, but it was best for her at the time." I hadn't thought of it quite that way before, and his words have stayed with me.

You did what was best for you at the time—your way of preserving your agency; your way of staying free. I think of this quote from Seneca, who killed himself in 65 AD, a quote that gave me chills when I first read it: "From each branch liberty hangs. Your neck, your throat, your heart are all so many ways of escape from slavery . . . Do you enquire the road to freedom? You shall find it in every vein of your body." You did what you thought was best for yourself, and even though it may have come out strangely at times over the years, I know you always tried to do what you thought was best for your girls.

Thank you for all you've given me. My life. The world. Faith in creativity, in justice. Love. So very much love.

I love you, Mom. That's never stopped; it never will.

Always and forever,
Your Gayley

[A candle flickers next to these words:]

Eleanor Roosevelt said "It is better to light
a candle than to curse the darkness."

It is my wish for this documentary to bring
many struggling patients out of the darkness
of misdiagnosis.

   —Arlene Baylen Brandeis

[The candle fades slowly to black.]

Epilogue

SEPTEMBER 26, 2012

I drop Hannah off at a television taping in Van Nuys that runs from two to seven, a sketch-comedy pilot featuring Bob Odenkirk, one of her heroes. She's excited, and I am, too—Michael is home with Asher, who will be three in a couple of months; I've brought my laptop, and plan to find a place where I can plunk myself down and write like a fiend for the next five hours. I zero in on a tea house with great reviews on Yelp, but when I pass the address, I realize the shop's inside a big mall and I've missed the entrance for the parking garage. After I round the corner to find another way inside, I wind up in the lane that pours onto the freeway. Something in me rises up and says, *Maybe I'm not supposed to go to the tea place. Maybe I'm supposed to get on the freeway and drive to South Pasadena; maybe I'm supposed to visit Golden Oaks.* The thought makes my blood sputter, but it also feels clear and whole and true. Writing can wait. I know exactly where I need to go.

I've considered a pilgrimage to Golden Oaks many times—on my way home from readings, on my way to museums; any time, really, I drive near Pasadena—but it's never felt like the right moment. Today is different. I don't have to be anywhere for hours. I am alone. Plus, it's August 30th, thirty-three months to the day that we got word of her death. This feels significant; thirty-three was my favorite number for years. As much as I hated 333 Hibbard Road as a teenager, I loved all the 3s. And I'm starting out in Van Nuys, home of the police station that first dealt with my mom's missing person's case.

I pull onto the eastbound 101, follow it onto the 134, tap the address for the Golden Oaks Apartments into my phone for directions when traffic comes to a stall.

Can I do this? I keep asking myself. *Am I up to this?* Nothing in me says *No,* at least not too loudly, at least not louder than the part that says *Yes,* so I keep moving forward.

I drive past Suicide Bridge, a gorgeous old span of Beaux Arts arches that curves by the freeway in Pasadena. Its official name is the Colorado Street Bridge, but dozens of people have jumped from it since it was built in 1912—the majority during the Depression years. A suicide barrier was eventually erected, but the nickname stuck. I wonder how many survivors have journeyed to its concrete pillars, how many have stood under the globe lights, pressed themselves against the railing and imagined their loved ones hurtling themselves over the edge.

I should buy some flowers, I decide. An offering. A bit of beauty to leave behind.

My heart starts to pound as my exit comes into view. I keep my eye out for a florist as I drive down Fair Oaks with no luck; then I see a nursery, a lovely urban jungle, and make a quick left turn.

The day is hot, the scent of vegetation thick in the air. I wander amongst the rows of plants, hoping the riot of life will fortify me for where I'm about to go.

Remember this, I tell myself. *Remember this green.*

Dark purple grapes drip from an arbor; I make sure nobody's watching, then pick one and pop it into my mouth as I walk, the bitterness of its skin giving way to a flood of sweet. *Remember this, too,* I tell myself.

I finally find the section with roses, my eye trained for yellow, my mom's favorite. I spy a bush full of sunny fist-sized blossoms, but when I try to pick it up, the large plastic pot won't move—the roots have anchored themselves into the soil below. A couple of rows down, I find a smaller bush with one perfect yellow rose rising from it like a torch. I picture clipping that rose and leaving it on the floor of the Golden Oaks parking garage, planting the bush at home later as a living memorial for my mom. Then I remember my lousy track record with plants; I know watching this one die will fill me with guilt. I decide to leave a note with the pot and hope some resident will find it and choose to care for it.

The tag lashed to the bush says these roses are *heirloom*—a word that somehow feels appropriate—but it also says they are magenta, not yellow. I wonder aloud if the roses will somehow deepen into red as they grow, but the guy at the counter takes a look and says, "This is wrong." He strokes his lip in thought. "I don't think they're Julia Childs," he says, and I have a sudden memory of my mom doing her Julia Child impersonation. "Skim the scum," she would trill, her favorite line from *The French Chef*, taken from an episode where Julia makes chicken stock. The man walks across the room, grabs a book of yellow rose varietals, and brings it back to the counter. I crane my head to read all the names beneath bright photos of roses as he flips through the pages, saying, "Not this, not this, not this"—names like Buttercream and Michelangelo and Easy Going. I find myself hoping the rose I picked will have one of the names related to gold—Gold Medal, Midas Touch, even Ch-Ching—so it will resonate with Golden Oaks, with my mom's quest for gold, but the guy isn't aware of my desire for narrative cohesion. "Sun Flare," he says, tapping the page. "I think it's Sun Flare."

The Sun Flare sits on the seat next to me in the car, the single rose bobbing like it's listening to music, or maybe davening in Jewish prayer. I cut though a residential area filled with storybook houses, and turn right onto El Centro, the street listed on the death certificate. My own center is buzzing. *Can I do this? I can do this. Can I do this?*

I drive past a park with a Mediterranean-style recreation center across the street from an old school district building with an arched walkway. The neighborhood is tree-lined, friendly-looking, and this gives me some comfort. The road is closed up ahead, though, right where the address should be, and I feel a surge of panic, imagining a police blockade. Did they block off the street when they took my mom's body away? Has it been closed all this time? It takes me a moment to realize there's a farmer's market behind the barricades. A farmers' market directly in front of Golden Oaks. I can't help but smile; I was expecting to confront my mom's death here in a somber, private way, no one around to intrude on my important moment, but life greets me here in abundance. Heaps of fruit gleam inside the bustling stalls. I park across the street and scoop the Sun Flare from the passenger seat. I'm a little shaky, but also strangely calm underneath, the sort of calm that washes through me when I know I'm where I'm supposed to be.

A flower stand is set right in front of the entrance to the building; I could have bought a bouquet for my mom on site. My heart sinks a bit to see that behind the buckets of gladiolas and Gerber daisies, Golden Oaks is not as luxurious as I had imagined. It has more of a Residence Inn vibe than any sort of Ritz-Carlton poshness. The walls are painted a brownish stucco, the fencing a stark white metal. The dated sign at the corner says "Welcome Home," words that echo inside my ribcage, horrible and sweet. The sign also reminds me Golden Oaks is a senior living community, a fact I had somehow forgotten. I wonder if my dad would ever consider living here, if it would help him feel closer to my mom. He's often said that he never wants to go anywhere near Los Angeles again, but recently decided to "get over himself" so he could consider going to my cousin's upcoming wedding in Pasadena, not far from here.

I lug the Sun Flare around the entire block-long perimeter of the building, squeezing through the barricades that cut off access to the alley where bakery stand workers smoke on their break, before I find the entrance to the parking garage. The long sliding gate is locked. I tug at its white metal bars but it only moves a smidgen, clanging against its frame. How did my mom get inside? I look down the ramp into the dim garage. The last place my mom ever walked. Was she running, frantic, as she made her descent? Did she know what she was about to do?

I don't know what to do, myself. I consider leaving the Sun Flare next to the gate, whispering a blessing through the bars, but this doesn't feel like enough. I find myself on auto-pilot, walking back to the front of the building, traveling up the half-circle driveway that reminds me of the curved driveway in front of my childhood apartment building, the driveway where my sister and I performed *Annie* on roller skates for our neighbors. I never imagined I would go into the building itself, but here I am. The glass door says "Push," but when I do, nothing happens. I peer inside; the place looks dishearteningly institutional, but there's a nice sitting room across the foyer, filled with model-home-style furniture my mom would like.

"Want me to punch in the code?" an older woman sitting on a bench by the entrance asks.

"That would be great, thank you," I tell her; she smiles and heads to the keypad. I probably look like I'm here to visit my grandmother, give her some roses for her balcony; for a split second, I let myself believe that's what I'm about to do, even though I haven't had a grandparent since I was six.

I thank the woman again as the door unlocks and wonder if she knows about my mom. How would her expression change if she knew who I was, why I was there?

The entrance is a big open foyer, like something in a hospital or office building. A white board on the wall advertises the movie they're showing to residents that night: *The Perfect Family*. A hard little laugh explodes in my chest.

I turn the corner and enter the open door of the office. A woman is sitting at a desk by the window, the only source of light in the dim room. I have no idea what to say.

"I'm here for sort of a strange reason," I begin as I walk toward her, and then I start to cry. I hadn't known the tears were coming, but of course they were there, waiting for the right moment. The woman stands up from her desk. She is Asian, middle-aged, a bit tired-looking, washed out like her gray t-shirt.

"My mother took her own life in this building almost three years ago," I say.

"I wasn't here," she says curtly, and I immediately wish I hadn't come inside, hadn't said a thing. Then her face softens; she says, "I was on vacation in Chicago" and something in me softens, too. Chicago, where my mom was born. Where I was born. "I got a call from police; they told me a resident hanged herself."

"She wasn't a resident," I say, but of course she knows this. She comes up to me and gives me a hug, a slightly stiff hug, like the kind my mom would often give me. It feels both wonderful and frustrating all at once—like my mom's hugs.

She laughs nervously as she pulls away, then says, "I got your e-mail."

I had sent an e-mail over a year ago through the Golden Oaks website, introducing myself and asking how my mom's death had affected the community. No one ever wrote back.

"You're a writer, right, and you live in Riverside?"

I nod, feeling strangely exposed.

"I didn't know what to tell you," she says. "The residents here were scared. They thought she was homeless. They didn't feel safe."

I am suddenly hungry to hear her story. Every nerve in my body is primed for it. I have been so stuck in my own version of my mom's death; the prospect of hearing another angle opens new space inside me.

"But I tell them no, she was an elegant lady, with a scarf, and a family." She sweeps her hand down her body, as if showing off a magnificent shawl. "And they tell me their hearts hurt for her. For you."

I nod, tears streaming down my face. Nodding seems to be all I can do.

"I light a candle for her there," she says. "For her peace."

"Wow," I say, still nodding, my hand now on my chest. "Thank you."

"The landlords, they're Chinese," she says, and I wonder if her family is Chinese, as well. "They brought in a Buddhist master. I don't believe it, but they wanted him to clear the space."

All of this, the candle, the Buddhist master, feels like food, the way my body is taking it in. I can almost feel my blood-sugar spike. I need this. I need this story.

"He told them the light led her here," she says. "Not like lights, but *light*." She makes another gesture, like she's pulling taffy out to her sides, and I somehow know just what she means. I'm not sure I believe it, either, but who knows? Who knows how my mom ended up in this place?

I realize my arms have started to ache from the heft of the Sun Flare. "I brought these flowers." I hoist them a bit higher, biceps straining. "I don't know what to do with them. They were my mom's favorite."

"Leave them here." She gestures to an area by her desk. "I can plant them in the courtyard." Suddenly the fact that I ended up at a nursery makes perfect sense. We wouldn't have been able to plant a bouquet. I gently lower the pot to the floor, and my arms feel instantly light, as if they are going to float right out of their sockets.

"Can I see it?" I ask, and she leads me through the sitting room, with its leather chairs and abstract art, out to a small courtyard with a fountain. The sky is gray, humid; its presses against my skin as if it wants to help hold me up. The iron patio furniture is covered with burnt-orange colored cushions, one of my mom's favorite colors—the color she chose for my childhood couch, the color she chose for the stairway carpet in Winnetka, the color she often wore. A few planters contain geraniums and sage. No roses, but the Sun Flare will feel right at home.

"Are we standing over the garage?" I ask, my body filled with a sudden charge.

She nods. "Do you want to go down there?"

"No," shoots out of my mouth before I have a chance to think. I realize I don't need to see where she died. Being right here, feeling the space vibrating under my feet is enough. Knowing her favorite flower will bloom above it is enough.

When we walk back to the office, I notice a large flat screen on the wall by the door, filled with a grid of images from twelve different security cameras. Two shots of the garage are in the bottom row, grainy and gray. The woman sees where I'm looking.

"She came down here," she says, pointing to the ramp. "She came in right after a car came out."

So that's how she got past the locked gate. I hold my breath.

"That was around 4:30, 4:50," she says. "The sanitation guy found her around 7:30 the next morning." I find myself grateful it wasn't an elderly resident, although I'm sure it was traumatic for the worker. I wonder who he's told the story to, how the image still haunts him.

"She looks calm in the video," she tells me, her voice kind. "I hope that helps. She was walking very calm, like she lived here. Like she knew exactly where she was going."

"That does help," I say, a new sense of peace flooding through me. "I'm glad she looked calm."

"Calm and elegant," she says. "She walked straight to the room and closed the door behind her." She makes a gesture as if she is closing double doors with both hands, but there is just a single door on the screen. It is white, and it glows, a luminous rectangle in a sea of gray. The light that led her here.

As soon as I step outside, it starts to rain, a soft, warm drizzle on my arms and face.

I had thought visiting Golden Oaks would bring me to my knees. I thought I would be wrecked by it; I thought I would be weeping so hard, I wouldn't be able to see the road as I drove away. I never imagined I would leave feeling so light, so clear, rain delicious on my skin.

The farmers' market is starting to close; people are packing up their stalls, putting peaches and hummus and honey into big plastic bins. I find myself heading straight for the Homeboy Bakery booth, find myself gravitating toward a loaf of yeasted pumpkin-pecan bread. I purchase it, then go to the next stall over and buy a pint of fresh pomegranate-orange juice.

The rain is really starting to come down, so I race to the car with my small bounty. I sit in the driver's seat for a while, water seeping into my shirt, realizing that I can see the gate to the garage from where I'm parked. I open the bag of bread and take out a slice. The top is sticky with brown sugar glaze, the bread itself—the same color as the patio chairs in the courtyard—sweet and satisfying. I open the juice, take a big swig and wonder if anything has ever tasted so good. Later, when I tell Michael about the day, he'll say, "It sounds like communion, the bread and juice." This doesn't occur to me in any conscious way at the time, but I feel it, feel a sense of communion as I chew and sip and swallow and stare at the white metal gate, my mother's last passage.

My sister-in-law Magdalene recently said, "She was an operatic person. It was an operatic way to go." I hadn't been able to take those words in fully at the time, but now I feel that aria, that crescendo. I feel the strange majesty of the act, which both startles and comforts me.

The Mayans believed suicide by hanging was an honorable way to die. The goddess Ixtab would accompany the hanged, along with warriors who died in battle and women who died in childbirth, to paradise, where she would serve them food beneath the leafy shade of the World Tree. I wonder what she fed them; bread and juice, perhaps. I raise my plastic bottle in the direction of the gate before I pull away from the curb, leaving part of my mother behind at Golden Oaks, flaring like the sun.

Resources

More than eight hundred thousand people take their own lives worldwide every year. That's one suicide every eight seconds. In America, a person commits suicide every thirteen minutes. Eight hundred thousand moments of desperation a year; eight hundred thousand hearts intentionally stilled. Millions of loved ones left to grapple with confusion and regret and anger, with the particularly complicated grief that suicide leaves in its wake.

When my mom died, I felt so isolated; I couldn't remember knowing anyone who had lost a loved one to suicide. Since then, I've learned that many people I know had faced such loss; since then, some of my closest friends have themselves lost loved ones to suicide.

It helps to know we are not alone. It helps to talk about suicide loss, to take this often stigmatized grief out of the shadows, to give it air and light so we can process, so we can heal, so we can let go of lingering ghosts of shame.

The American Foundation for Suicide Prevention sponsors the annual International Suicide Survivors Day in November, with events around the world (http://www.survivorday.org). They also organize annual Out of the Darkness walks (https://www.afsp .org/out-of-the-darkness-walks), and can help you find a suicide -loss survivors' support group at https://www.afsp.org/coping-with -suicide-loss/find-support/find-a-support-group.

The American Association of Suicidology offers resources for people coping with suicide loss, including an annual Healing After Suicide conference (http://www.suicidology.org/suicide-survivors /suicide-loss-survivors).

Some survivors of suicide loss are tempted to end their own lives. If you are feeling suicidal, help is available. The Suicide Prevention Hotline can be reached at (800) 273-TALK (8255).

Seek out the resources that speak to you and what you need most directly and clearly. None of us have the exact same path, but we can help shed light along one another's journey through grief.

Let's keep talking. Let's stop hiding this loss. We are many, and we can help each other live.

Acknowledgments

This is the hardest, most necessary book I've ever written, and there were many times I wasn't sure I was up for the challenge. I'm so grateful to everyone who kept me and my work moving forward.

Thank you deeply to everyone who read early sections and drafts of the manuscript and offered invaluable advice and support: Laraine Herring, Rebecca O'Connor, Elizabeth Aamot, Susan Ito, Ellen Geiger, Bernadette Murphy, Suzanne Roberts, Cindy Bokma, Renee Sedliar. Special thanks to Arielle Bernstein, who generously read several drafts of the memoir and greatly informed its evolution. You are all goddesses.

Tremendous gratitude to Julie Greicius at the *Rumpus*, Jennifer Pastiloff and Angela Giles Patel at the *Manifest-Station*, Jennifer Niesslein at *Full Grown People*, Sarah Hepola at *Salon*, Elizabeth Cohen at the *Saranac Review*, Erika Kleinman at the *Nervous Breakdown*, and Rebecca Rubenstein at *Midnight Breakfast* for publishing (and helping shape) portions of the memoir. Thank you, too, to everyone who shared these essays online and wrote to me directly—you helped me realize my story could reach beyond myself.

Workshops with Lidia Yuknavitch, Emily Rapp, and Saeed Jones generated material that ended up in this book—thank you all for your fierce and vital inspiration. I also wrote several scenes during in-class writing time in my workshops at Sierra Nevada College and am grateful to my students for being so kind as I shared very raw work (I'm also wildly grateful to June Saraceno for changing my life by bringing me to Sierra Nevada College). Thank you to all my current and former students and colleagues at both SNC and Antioch University Los Angeles (and at workshops I've taught around the country)—you are such gifts in my life.

I am thankful beyond words for my agent, Christopher Rhodes (and my friend Peter Selgin for connecting us). Your insight and guidance and encouragement helped make this a better book, and you found the perfect home for it at Beacon Press, with the perfect editor, Amy Miller Caldwell. Amy, thank you for understanding my vision so deeply and using your thoughtful, thorough eye to help me hone it. Everyone at Beacon has been a joy to work with—thank you all from the bottom of my heart.

Thank you to the amazing writers who wrote blurbs for the book; your kind words take my breath away.

Thank you to my therapist, Laura Cueva-Miller, for suggesting I write to my mom—it was transformational for both me and the structure of this book. The writing retreat at St. Mary's Art Center in Virginia City was also transformational; thank you to all the women who were there—you helped midwife this memoir in so many ways.

Thank you to all my dear friends—too many to name—who called and wrote and brought food and comfort after my mom's death. You were such important lifelines. Special thanks to Nancy Tedder and Jennifer Vallely for being such loving, wise grief doulas during that painful time, and to Jane O'Shields-Hayner, Bill Hayner, and Cati Porter for holding me and my family in so many ways.

My family. How can I thank you enough? Michael and my kids, Arin, Hannah, and Asher—you are my greatest treasures, and I love you all with every fiber of my being. Sue and Jon, you and your wonderful spouses, Larry and Magdalene, walked through this experience with us with so much love and grace and strength; I am so lucky to be your sister. Thank you to Cousin Bobby for flying out to support us and our dad (and thank you to all our other relatives who reached out, with special thanks to my brother-in-law, Craig, and my neice, Mo. What a beautiful *mishpucha*.) Dad—I miss you so much. Thank you for always supporting me and my writing; thank you for leaving such a legacy of love. Elizabeth. Elizabeth. How could I have gotten through this without you? You have been at the heart of my life since the day you were born, the day my memories began. I know how hard my writing this book has been for you, and I'm so grateful for your ultimate understanding, your ultimate blessing. You are my anchor, my sister of blood and bone and gut and heart; you are my everything.